Women and Islamization

Women and Islamization

Contemporary Dimensions of Discourse on Gender Relations

**Edited by
Karin Ask and Marit Tjomsland**

Oxford • New York

First published in 1998 by
Berg
Editorial offices:
150 Cowley Road, Oxford, OX4 1JJ, UK
70 Washington Square South, New York, NY 10012, USA

Berg is the imprint of Oxford International Publishers Ltd.

Library of Congress Cataloging-in-Publication Data

A catalogue record for this book is available from the Library of Congress

British Library Cataloguing-in-Publication Data

A catalogue record for this book is available from the British Library

ISBN   1 85973 250 X (Cloth)
        1 85973 255 0 (Paper)

Printed in the United Kingdom by Biddles Ltd, Guildford and King's Lynn

Contents

Preface

The idea to write this book originates from a seminar organized around the theme *Construction of Gender Relations in Processes of Modernization: Women and Islamization* at the Chr.Michelsen Institute in Bergen, Norway. The seminar received funding from the Norwegian Research Council for Science and the Humanities and the Norwegian Ministry of Foreign Affairs co-sponsored the work on editing and publication of the book. We gratefully acknowledge the financial support received from the above-mentioned agencies and institution.

Much of the material has been changed since the original seminar, and some of the participants who presented papers and contributed to the development of arguments in the seminar in late 1994 have for various reasons been unable to publish their papers in this volume. We would like to thank Trude Eide, Aynur Ilyasoglu, Kirsten Sandborg, Heidi Skramstad and Annika Rabo for their contribution to the discussions in the seminar which encouraged our further work on the various draft manuscripts towards publication. The chapters in this volume written by Marjo Buitelaar, Wilhelmina Jansen and Soroya Duval have been included by invitation.

The different chapters of the book grapple with understanding the phenomena that in Western popular and scholarly discourse often are presented under the label 'religious fundamentalism'. By investigating the positive variety of religious practice in a smaller number of case studies we seek to describe religion as something that takes place in everyday life and thereby is actively founded in the experiences of the believing woman. Implicitly we question what unites these beliefs and groups apart from *our* ascription of a specific negatively defined identity to them by the attributes non-modern, non-democratic, irrational.

A unifying approach for the different papers presented at the seminar was to analyze ways in which Muslim women develop distinct voices and participate in Islamization processes. The empirical cases presented highlight the creation of rooms for religious reflections and devotion, public meeting and discourse by the women engaged in Islamist resurgence.

In the cases presented and the questions raised, we try to conceptualize religion in ways that contest descriptions of women's relation to Islam as being universally its victims.

The chapters in this book draw upon fieldwork in different Muslim communities and include terminology from a number of different languages, namely Arabic, Persian, Turkish and Wolof. The material presented incorporates colloquial as well as literary usages. This poses considerable problems of transliteration and no attempts has been made towards a standardized presentation throughout the book, except for recurring words like the Koran. The editors have, however, sought to observe uniformity of spelling and style within the individual chapters. We have also sought as far as possible to omit the use of diacritics.

Notes on Contributors

Karin Ask is a social anthropologist and research fellow at Chr. Michelsens institute. She has been doing basic and applied research in Afghanistan, Bangladesh and Pakistan. Her publications include: 'Veiled experiences: Exploring female practices of seclusion' in Kirsten Hastrup & Peter Hervik (eds), *Social Experience and Anthropological Knowledge* (1994, London: Routledge) and 'Ishq aur Mohabbat: contrastive ideas on love and friendship in a northern Pakistani Community' in T. Bleie, V. Broch-Due and I. Rudie, (eds), *Carved Flesh/Cast Selves: Gendered Symbols and Social Practices* (1993, Oxford: Berg).

Marjo Buitelaar is a cultural anthropologist and works as assistant professor at the Centre for Religious Studies of the State University of Groningen, The Netherlands. She is active in research and teaches on the subject of Anthropology of the Middle East and Islam. She has published numerous articles in Dutch and English on women in muslim culture and society. Among recent publications are 'Widow's worlds. Representations and realities' in J. Bremmer and L. van den Bosch, *Between Poverty and Pyre. Moments in the history of Widowhood* (1995, London & New York: Routledge) and 'Between oral tradition and literacy. Women's use of the holy scriptures in Morocco' in A. Fodor & A. Shivtiel (eds), *Proceedings and Colloquium on Popular Customs and the Monotheistic Religions in the Middle East and North Africa.* Special issue of The Arabist. Budapest Studies in Arabic 9-10, Budapest. She is the author of *Fasting and Feasting in Morocco. Women's Participation in Ramadan* (1993, Oxford: Berg).

Soroya Duval is a research fellow affiliated to the Department of Sociology at Lund University Sweden. She did fieldwork for her PhD. thesis in Sociology in Cairo among female participants in Islamic groups. She has published articles in Swedish and English for example 'Socio-economic effects of Labour Migration on Women and Children in Egypt' (1989) in Research Report Series Department of Sociology, Lund.

Wilhelmina Jansen is professor of women's studies and director of the Centre of Women's studies at the University of Nijmegen. Her main anthropological research was done in Algeria, which resulted in the book *Women without men. Gender and Marginality in an Algerian town* (1987, Leiden: E.J. Brill). Her current research deals with the history of women's education in Jordan, changes in gender identity during the life course and women's multiple identities.

Zahra Kamalkhani is a social anthropologist and research fellow at the Centre for Feminist Research in the Humanities at the University of Bergen, Norway. Among her recent publications are 'Women's Everyday religious discourse in Iran' in H. Afshar (ed.), *Women in the Middle East* (1994, London: Macmillan Press). Her PhD thesis *Women's Islam: Religious Practice among Women in Todays Iran* (1997) is forthcoming.

Catharina Raudvere is assistant professor and teaches history of religions at the Faculty of Philosophy, Linköping University. She has previously written on Old Norse mythology and Scandinavian folklore but has in the last years developed scholarly interest in Muslim groups in Turkey and is at present conducting fieldwork among female dervishes in Istanbul. Her disciplinary training is as an ethnofolklorist. Among her recent publications are 'Now you see her, now you don't: Some Notes on the Conceptions of Female Shape-shifters in Scandinavian tradition' in Sandra Billington and Miranda Green (eds) *The Concept of the Goddess* (1996). She has published on her present research in various articles, e.g. 'To decide her own way. Female Dervishes in Istanbul' (1996 in Swedish).

Anne Sofie Roald is a research fellow affiliated to the Department of Theology and Religious Studies at Lund University Sweden. Her doctoral dissertation is titled *Tarbiya: Education and Politics in Islamic Movements in Jordan and Malaysia* (1992, Lund Studies in History of Religions, Vol. 3).

Eva Evers Rosander is senior research fellow at the Nordic Africa Institute in Uppsala, Sweden and Associate Professor in Social Anthropology. She has done extensive fieldwork in northern Morocco and Ceuta on women and social and economic change. Recently she has been studying Sufi women (Murids) in Senegal and their religious associations. She has published *Women in a Borderland. Managing Muslim Identity where Morocco meets Spain* (1991, Stockholm SSSA). Together with David Westerlund she has edited a book on *African - Islam: Encounters between Sufis and Islamists* (1997, London: Hurst and Uppsala: Nordic Africa Institute).

Marit Tjomsland is a sociologist and NFR stipendiate at the Chr. Michelsen Institute, currently working on Islamism and social modernization in Tunisia. Among her publications are 'The Educated Way of Thinking: Individualisation and Islamism in Tunisia' in M. Masst, T. Hylland Eriksen and J. Helle-Valle (eds), *State and Locality* (1994) and *A Discussion of Three Theoretical Approaches to Modernity: Understanding Modernity as a Globalising Phenomenon* in CMI Working Paper series 1996.

Introduction

Karin Ask and Marit Tjomsland

This book describes how Muslim women in various national settings contribute to the Islamization of their societies. Focusing on the dissimilarity in religious practice between women, we emphasize how being a Muslim woman is always marked by differences of national culture, education, class and age. Our objective is to present religion as 'something that actually takes place in human life' by descriptions of religious belief, practices, motivations and perceptions among women.

The chapters that follow are based upon participatory research among women in Muslim communities from Senegal in the West to Iran in the East. The authors seek to specify the complex relationship between gender and Islam through analyses of ethnographic cases that highlight the place of religious devotion and piety in women's lives. The studies presented comprise descriptions of female members in Islamist groups, women who transmit and recreate traditional religious rituals, young girls as preachers educated in state sponsored religious educational institutions and those who mainly contribute to the public reformulation of Islamic traditions by changes in their personal modes of comportment. We do not enter into explicit discussion of the comparative and systemic literature on fundamentalism searching for structural commonalities in the intersection between religion and gender, but explore some of the transformational links between women's religious practice and dominant religious discourse. When the term 'fundamentalism' is used, it is related to individual clarifications and arguments in Chapters 1 and 3. Otherwise our analysis is confined to discursive practices *within*

Islam, where the terms used are 'Islamism' and 'Islamist practices'.

In the book *The Failure of Political Islam* (1994), Olivier Roy argues that radical Islamic movements of the 1970s and 1980s have entered into a new phase characterized by a popular re-Islamization on a grassroots level, where movements branch into society in ways that penetrate everyday life and political discourse. The immediate target of the policy is no longer to establish Islamic society through state power, but to conquer the society through 'reform of mores (that) centres on the return to individual religious practice' (ibid.: 79). These movements involve a vast number of activities that are considered to promote public virtue and the maintenance of personal piety.

The Islamization of society develops along two main axes: individual reform through preaching (*dawa*), and the establishment of Islamized space. We describe these processes in a gendered perspective and emphasize women's contribution to both; how they critically engage the regulatory discourse that marks their bodies and voices by habitual forms of gender subordination. 'Islamization of space' refers to attempts to 're-Islamize' society by encouraging individuals to practice Islam in daily life and bridge the gap between religious discourse and practical realities through prayer, fasting, segregation of space between the two genders, veiling of women and so on. Thus, Islamization from the 'bottom up' does not necessarily entail asking women to return to the home, but rather that the sexes are separated in public.

In the West, scholarly and popular debates tend to presume that there is only one authoritative Islamist agenda on women and Islam — the opposite is closer to the truth. The lack of a universal policy among Muslim states who claim to follow religious law (*Sharia*) in respect of women's rights is remarkable — in Iran women vote, and a women - Dr. Ebtekar - has just taken up the post as vice president of the republic, all of which is unthinkable in the traditionalist Saudi monarchy. While the scope of argument in the articles do not warrant any generalization about the development of an indigenous feminist movement in Muslim states (cf. Yamani 1996: 24), the ethnographic cases presented support the view of Lisa Taraki who argues that this is the 'one area of the Islamist agenda which is most open to debate and most amenable to experimentation' (1996: 159 - 178).

Religious organization of cults and practices is an important site for the social construction of gender ideology, and the positions taken by women is consequential to both sexes, whether they consent to consent to dominant models, reformulate them or actively oppose them. Women's roles in contemporary Islamic resurgence has largely been analyzed within a resistance model - where they often appear as the victims of reactionary male fanatics. We try to open for explanations of female participation in Islamization that go beyond interpretations that use categories of victimization and false consciousness. This is not to say that analytical perspectives on subordination and resistance are invalid, but rather that the choice of explanatory factors and focus have tended to blur and exclude the factors showing a general strengthening of female Muslim identity. Thus, in what follows we describe how women participate in processes where normative ideology is opened up in ways that enlarge their room to manoeuvre and explore some of the ways in which they bridge gaps between everyday practical realities and religious discourse.

Islamization often includes the adaption of certain 'universal' Islamic cultural forms and practices, notably changes in the female dress code; donning the veil (Arabic *hijab*) by women is to Western eyes most conspicuous, and is often interpreted as an icon of return to orthodox Islamic traditions. The relevance of these changes in environment for women depends upon the particular mix between universalizing forms and local traditions and practices. The Islamization described in the present case studies concentrate on phenomena where women are the critical mediators and interpreters of Islamization in everyday life. The women described are largely involved in religious practices that are classified as popular (or low) Islam. However, in the cases from Egypt and Iran, we are introduced to intellectual Islamist women who write, publish and otherwise make their individual voices heard in the theological debates on women and religion. The contributions of both these categories of women warrant our attention if we are to gain an understanding of who sets the agenda and what is the appeal of Islamist ideology for women.

In the book *Postmodernism, Reason and Religion* (1992), Ernest

Gellner suggests that the current revitalization of religion in modernizing Muslim societies, which contradicts the conventional perception of secularization as a central aspect of modernity, may be explained in terms of the ancient division between the scripturalist 'high Islam' of the scholars and elites and the less correct 'low Islam' of the unlearned masses. The relationship between these two versions of Islam has, according to Gellner, historically never been dynamic. 'High Islam's' repeated attempts at converting the adherents of 'low Islam' have only temporarily been successful, as tradition and folk belief always have reconquered the minds of the masses and brought the process back to square one. The current modernization of Muslim societies is, however, on the verge of finally ending this infertile circle, as it is removing what 'low Islam' has been feeding on for centuries — traditional thought and society. This is, according to Gellner, the background to the astonishing strength and vitality of Islamism — as the current most vital expression of 'high Islam'. Modernization decreases that part of the population inclined to identify with 'low Islam', but since 'high Islam' provides a more sophisticated religious interpretation attractive to the growing modernized section of the population, Islam does not suffer from secularization as other religions have done as a result of modernization.

Gellner's analysis contains insights that may contribute to an understanding of the ongoing processes of Islamization in general and the specific expressions of such processes presented here. Nevertheless, the analysis needs modification. When relating to the concepts of 'high' and 'low' Islam, it is important to bear in mind that they are constructs, and actual content will fluctuate with movements in the empirical field they refer to. Moreover, these concepts have advocates in two separate camps. They are used both by researchers approaching Islam from an external secular point of view and by learned guardians of 'high Islam' within the context of believers, but in different ways and according to different preconditions, which further complicates the picture. Hence, Gellner's claim that 'low Islam' resulting from modernization is permanently giving way to 'high Islam' is rather problematic.

This is not to deny that modernization is bringing about

significant changes in religious consciousness and practice in Muslim societies. Increased geographical mobility removes the organization of religious life from its traditional local community contexts. Increased access to formal education enables individual Muslims to access the religious sources, and mass media expose even the illiterate to a wider range of religious impulses — reducing the importance of local religious leaders as sole guardians of religious truth. Such changes weaken social mechanisms which have been important for the maintenance of 'low Islam' for centuries, and may therefore apparently support Gellner's argument.

However, a number of the cases presented in this book suggest that such social changes, in spite of their weakening effect on ancient social mechanisms, do not necessarily result in a final eradication of 'low Islam'. Indeed, they may lead to a redefinition of the social basis of 'low Islamic' practices (Raudvere, Evers Rosander, Kamalkhani, this volume).

As modernization evolves, it brings about new problems and tensions. Increased generational conflicts challenge traditional structures of authority, and accentuate tensions between individual priorities and collective expectations. Urbanization detaches individuals from their original local contexts, and challenges them to construct their life according to new preconditions. Moreover, such changes tend to affect women's lives more than men's, due to the conventionally heavier control of their conduct, and the higher expectations that they lead their lives within the realms of the family, and according to the family's needs and priorities rather than their own. This book presents analyses of how Muslim women in very different ways include religion in their strategies for coping with such problems. Some of the cases describe contemporary revivals of what one may term traditional 'low Islamic' elements in the religious practices of Muslim women as they strive to carve a space for themselves in modernizing Muslim societies. Maintenance of traditional popular religious associations and practices within a modern social context appears to provide these women with a counterweight to the strains of modernity. Other contributors describe women within new religious organizations which have sprung into existence as a result of the current process of Islamization, and which include religious practices which are new, but all the same more easily associated with 'low' than with 'high' Islam.

Thus, while it is clear that social modernization brings about change in religious practices, it is not at all clear that such changes will necessarily be directed away from 'low Islamic' practices. Neither is it clear that the conceptual dichotomy of 'low' and 'high' Islam provides a particularly well suited analytical framework for studies of this kind of change. Thus, instead of attempting to categorize the contributions according to this dichotomy, we want to draw attention to the great *heterogeneity* which characterizes these cases of Islamization. In our view, it is the very different nature of these accounts of Muslim women's relationship to the phenomenon of Islamization that makes a presentation of them interesting, as it argues against prevailing rigid images of both Muslim women and Islamization. Furthermore, this heterogeneity provides a better entry to a discussion of the relationship between Islamization and modernity than the one provided by Gellner, as it is variation and difference rather than uniformity and homogeneity which constitute central characteristics of modern societies in our time. However, this is a discussion which the authors only engage in here to a limited degree. That is, they all consider modernization to be a main catalyst for Islamization, but as they tend to opt for an emic approach to their respective fields of study, their analyses are not developed for the purpose of high level theoretical generalizations.

The cases presented in this book cover a wide range of Muslim women's involvement in current processes of Islamization. They include women's engagement in the creation of feminist Islamist theology on a sophisticated intellectual level (Roald, Chapter 1); women's activist engagement as leaders of women's religious associations which have sprung into existence as local expressions of Islamization (Duval, Chapter 2); women's involvement in support-groups for Islamist movements dominated by men (Duval, Chapter 2); and women's maintenance and recreation of traditional Sufi-based associations anchored in old popular forms of worship (Raudvere, Chapter 5; Evers Rosander, Chapter 6). Some of the contributions focus on individual women's motivations for changing their life-style in accordance with new interpretations of Islam (Jansen, Chapter 3). However, in spite of the large differences, the cases have a few very important common traits. It seems clear in them all that women's involvement results from personal choices, as part of their active moulding of modes of life which suit their needs and expectations in new, modernizing realities. Furthermore, all the studies show a clear tendency of women's increased engagement in religious, cultural and social life outside the private realm, and in arenas which were earlier rendered unaccessible to them — whether they be physical spaces, such as the mosques, or intellectual arenas, such as learned theological debates. It can be argued that some of the women's religious associations described by the authors contribute very little to a new model of Muslim womanhood, as they cultivate conventional female virtues such as modesty, obedience, and self-sacrifice in relation to children and family. However, the fact that Muslim women today actively engage in public life associations in ways that were earlier unobtainable to them and on conditions they define and choose for themselves is in our view more significant than the specific characteristics of the associations they partake in when it comes to promoting women's empowerment in a long term perspective.

The new alternatives made available to Muslim women by the processes of Islamization do, however, evolve within the limits of their respective national and institutional frameworks. As this book contains ethnographic studies of great geographical heterogeneity, it also serves as a documentation of the impact of such frameworks on local expressions of Islamization. For instance, Chapter 7 describes how in Iran, the religious regime encourages women's participation in religious associations with roots in popular tradition, and offers women formal religious education which qualifies them for positions as religious leaders within such associations. The potential gains of participating in such associations are thus apparently significant. Chapter 5 shows that in Turkey the situation is quite the opposite, as organized traditional forms of popular worship in general and Sufi-movements in particular are partially banned. However, in spite of unfavourable institutional conditions these associations are currently experiencing a period of revival, which may indicate that in Turkey they play a quite different political and social role than in Iran. This is yet another aspect of the heterogeneity characterizing the phenomenon of Islamization on which we have wanted to focus in this book.

Thus, while the main drift of the scholarly literature concentrates on commonalities in the positions given to women in fundamentalist rhetoric and similarities in motivations among women who join religious fundamentalist movements, we shall restrict our attention to variation in form and practices where women commit themselves to Islamization processes, concentrating on descriptive approaches that complement the ethnographic picture. We do not intend to give an exhaustive review of current work here, but having delineated the ground covered in this volume, we will take a brief look at two fairly representative contributions to the debate. Both *Fundamentalism and Gender* (Hawley: 1994) and *Mixed Blessings* (Brink and Mencher: 1997) grapple with the vexed relationship between women and religious revival asking why and how they are involved; both compare different religious traditions they seek to specify common ground for the intersection between fundamentalism and gender.

The first book concentrates on women as representation, as objects for fundamentalist discourse, and the underlying reasons why primarily men are recruited to fundamentalist movements. Frustrations and disappointment with promises of modernity loom large in the explanations given, as do the theoretical representation of women in the ideology of the movements. Another commonality between the religious movements discussed is the continuous redefinition of self by drawing boundaries that protect and control women as symbols of the authentic and sacred community of believers. In the symbolic marking of boundaries between self and other they materialize as touchstones for the culturally uncontaminated (see Kandyoti 1991: 1-15). Another common suggestion is that women constitute 'the internal other' who must be controlled. In opposition to this Harris submits that the 'otherness argument' deflects attention from 'own un-examined ethnocentrism' (Harris in Hawley 1994: 29). The book concludes that different perspectives are likely to ensue when women, not men, speak the language of fundamentalism (ibid.: 143).

The second book (*Mixed Blessings*) does exactly that and uses a woman-centred approach that concentrates on women as historical subjects and provides meticulous and sensitive ethnographic details. The title of the book reflects the explanation given as to why women become members. The cases presented are differentiated between three categories — those where religious participation can benefit women substantially in various ways; those where women are struggling to gain autonomy within the constraints of fundamentalism; and those where women are oppressed by their religious participation but feel they have little choice (Mencher in Brink and Mencher 1997: 3). Of the five cases covering Muslim communities only one appears under the heading where women benefit from fundamentalism, and the conclusion drawn is that 'we cannot state categorically that fundamentalisms are good or bad or have a specific impact on women's status' (Brink in Brink and Mencher 1997: 240).

If the driving force of feminism is to strive for 'freedom from' and resistance to patriarchal domination how can we explain the positions taken by women engaging in Islamization who also claim to strive for 'freedom to'? (cf. Sagal and Yuval-Davis 1992). How do we explain the apparent contradictory behaviour of women who freely join religious movements with an ideology that works against changes in gender relations in the direction of more equality between women and men? This question has often been answered by using the category of 'false consciousness', where the actor emerges predominately as the victim of mystifying and obfuscating ideology. We suggest that the great variation in the ways women are involved in these processes can be more fruitfully examined by using another frame of reference. Rather than starting from commonalities in an all-encompassing hegemonic discourse we start from the margins of the debate where analysis of locally situated case studies helps us understand the difference and slippage between dominant discourse and individual perceptions and self-representations (cf. de Lauretis 1987: 10). The women presented draw on a number of discourses and take up a variety of subject positions where they invest and make emotional commitments in multiple, even mutually competing, discourses on gender and religious practice. Reading within this frame of reference invites reflection on the relationship between resistance and complicity in ways that emphasize gender specific experience as a historical process adopting the fundamental feminist notion that the personal is political (cf. Moore 1994: 64-5).

While as a group the authors do not share a particular theoretical approach and although each chapter of the book describes very different ethnographic material, there are points of contact between the contributions that provide a unified direction to the volume. All of them deal with the issue of women who engage in religious discursive practices that push against the patriarchal boundaries and carve out new spaces. We will now consider how the position of de Lauretis and Moore can help us to look beyond the categories of resistance, complicity or suppression towards a comprehension of the cases where concepts of empowerment, choice, individuation and identity inform our perception. To illustrate this, we examine focal points of the different contributions concerning aspects of individuation and female investment in extra domestic networks.

The use of the veil in one of its various local forms for example face-veil (*niqab*), shawl (*chador*) or enveloping cloak (*burqa*) is a recurring theme in the narratives of the female informants, as a symbol of personal investment in intensifying religious commit-ment and at the same time a public statement of identity in the larger social space. The female dressing and re-dressing regulate and is formative for the female informants, and the analysis reveals the disjuncture created between the dominant male ideology and female perceptions that express an alternative understanding providing a certain freedom of action and reflection. Female informants emphasize how they use the veil pragmatically to get room to manoeuvre, enlarge their scope of action and increase their independent mobility in the social world outside domestic boundaries, a strategy that is legitimized by religious authoritative discourse. In addition, the veil is also a symbol that summarizes much of the Western historical discourse on Islam, where women at various stages of the colonial and post-colonial political periods were used as 'the most visible marker of the differentness and inferiority of Islamic societies' (Ahmed 1992: 152). Moreover, it is a condensed and acknowledged symbol for the political strategy and ambition of Islamist movements. What are the motivations of the women who appear as the objects of these conflicting discourses? Why do women wear the veil, what meaning and value does it have for the woman, her interacting partners or the passers-by in a street? What is the multiple signification of personal religious commitment and how does it bolster or subvert traditional patriarchal control?

Veiling is nowhere explicitly prescribed in the Koran, and the various interpretations of the verses that deal with female clothing, are not conclusive. Women are instructed to 'guard their private parts and throw a scarf over their bosom' (K. 24: 31-2), while the explicit reference to the veil appears in a verse that states, 'When you ask any of the wives of the Prophet for something, ask from behind a curtain (*hijab*)' (K. 33: 54). For the individual woman the veil materializes as a public statement of personal commitment, and the language used to reflect upon her life before and after re-activating commitment to Islamic religious and ritual practices may draw upon images from Islamic tradition that make the divide between before and after appear more or less dramatic — from the woman who speaks of her life in terms of before and after her big *Jahiliya* (connoting estrangement from Islam; also used to refer to the historical pre-Muslim Arab society), to the narratives of gradual change implied by reorganizing lifestyle and shifting commitments between work outside the home and domestic duties. It is important to note that what is today commonly considered as women's Islamic dress is not traditional in the sense of a return to types of veil used before, but reflects innovation made by the younger generation of women who use change of clothing to accentuate their identity and response to a changing world, and thereby even create a resourceful place for themselves within that world. A consequence of this mode of communicating changed identity is to put the individual women in focus and create a distance where women reflect upon what may earlier have been taken for granted.

The veil is commanding on the personal level as well as on the inter-personal level. In the cases described, a veil is also a personal symbol in the way it does something to the woman's body. The physical and visual reality of women evokes, according to conventional Muslim discourse, the seductive power of her body with reference to potentially shameful and impure acts. In a traditional male-oriented tradition women who wear the veil and are secluded embody their family's social prestige and materialize as indexes of the honour of men related to them. The contemporary social context, where a woman may choose to wear the veil even against the custom in her immediate family, challenges conventional expectations and explanations of male control of female seclusion thereby indicating development of a certain independence and self-reliance that opposes traditional discourse. Furthermore, the automatic correlation between veil and female seclusion in the form of purdah no longer holds true when the links to dominant male ideology are subverted by women who use the veil to escape the confines of tradition and enhance their access to public space. The changing routines for bodily practices such as taking a bath together with other women also emerge as an indication of the destabilization and reformulation of tradition. Women's changing preferences concerning the use of traditional locations for gender privacy suggest an intriguing variance between increased freedom of movement for the individual woman and a decrease in the importance of all-female meeting places like the traditional public baths (*hammam*). Islamizing women are among those who prefer the use of the shower over the public bath. The changing use of private and public space also illustrates how women are negotiating the boundaries between men and women who are permitted to enter into marriage (*na-mahram*) and those who are not (*mahram*). The contributions converge in their description of how shifts in meaning in this sphere are related to a reordering of practical activities, spatial relations and domestic environments.

The introduction of an Islamic dress code by political rulers to signal their Islamist programme has often created active opposition by women, and the reaction acquires a distinctly different quality if appropriated in an oppositional discourse. During the rule of Zia ul-Haq in Pakistan the slogan *Chador aur Char Diwari* (lit. 'The veil and the four walls') was used to project the political programme for Islamization of society. Sarcastic comments from women pointed out that the morals and demeanour of women as well as men depended on self-control manifest in 'the purdah of the eyes' (*Ankhoon ki Purdah*) not in the outward signs of a conservative all-enveloping cloak (*burqa*). The difference between public symbol and private meaning is further demonstrated by the way in which individual women in the different case-studies choose to embody the concept of the good Muslim woman so as to allow room for autonomy of action and self-definition, not as a predetermined reflection of dominant religious discourses.

As noted in several cases, the new veiling is adapted as a practical necessity for women working outside the home, who need to move around and use public transport. The Islamic dress is both a declarative symbol in the public space and a mnemonic device for the person wearing the veil. The differences in personal meaning and public significance among women who wear the veil are lost if it is simply reduced to an index of Muslim women's oppression. The contributions to this volume show, on the one hand, how personal choice and variation indicate the development of achieved rather than ascribed status and, on the other hand, how boundaries are drawn between self and other in new ways that denote increased female agency. Where traditionally the veil was a symbol for male kin's control over 'their' women, contemporary justification and discursive practices emphasize female self-control and independence in ways which challenge the traditional position.

Several of the papers also contribute further knowledge to the set of ideas which constitute the theory of muted groups: how voices that have remained silent or 'relatively inarticulate', effectively 'mute' (Ardener 1975: xii) are gaining ground. This may in due course generate alternative readings. The ability to gain a voice in the religious sphere is particularly significant where the holy text, the Koran, is God's revealed Words and charged with divine blessing (*barakat*). Several of the contributions describe how women are active in networks where they earn religious merit, and seek blessing from beneficent forces of divine origin.

Overlapping domains of spiritual liberation and secular empowerment are carved by the female informants where they seek to demarcate what Islam is and what it ought to be. The traffic between these semantic domains differs in the cases we present — from the vocal Islamic alternatives advocated by Muslim feminists in Egypt and Iran, to the lower voices presented in other case-studies.

In the chapter by Evers Rosander we are given a detailed analysis of transactions between older women and younger men which circumvent the conventional prohibition against women chanting certain religious songs. The manner in which women contribute to the conversion of value from the secular sphere into religious merit in a ritual sphere exemplifies the mediation between convention and invention that characterizes the material in this book. Thus, the circulation of symbolic material creates networks of ceremonial exchange where religious message is given priority over gender segregation. In the case of Sufi networks this mediation may also convert ritual value into material goods.

Some women are able to draw on historical traditions where they define their identity and link it to a historical tradition of indigenous feminism and authorized authenticity in contrast to Western feminism. As noted by Leila Ahmed and others, two divergent strains of feminism exist in the Middle East, one tending to affiliate itself with Western models while the other seeks to shape a path of female subjectivity and affirmation within the terms of indigenous culture (1994: 174-9).

The analysis of the interaction between identity markers of sex and religion is challenging as they share qualities of what Bateson called hard-programmed truths (1972: 501), conceptualizations of identities that are close to the transferred categories of nature, the ontologically given. The freeing of individual identity from pre-determination by class, race and biological sex has been the banner for historical and contemporary movements of liberation, not least the struggle for women's emancipation in this century. The shifts in meaning in cultural construction of gender relations are a result both of reordering of practical activities and continuous struggle (political,intellectual and artistically) to reinterpret and transform cultural traditions. Non-modern models of the relation between the individual and her social surroundings are seen as representing vestiges of suppression of individual human rights, or the embodiment of cultural systems that subordinate the individual to the collective. Religious movements in the modern world seem on the surface to go against this process of liberation of the individual, by defending traditional value hierarchies against the attacks that leave the individual as the ultimate measure of values that can be agreed upon. The case-studies presented in this book describe how women through their religious activities develop positions that push against fixed traditional patriarchal forms of domination in several spheres. Personifying local voices in this way does not of course, resolve the dilemma of gender asymmetry in the practices and discourse of Islamization. However, reflection on the cases encourages analytical insights that challenge the unquestioning privileging of Western feminism as the final hegemonic answer to questions of asymmetry between the two genders.

References

Afkhami, M. (ed.) (1995), *Faith & Freedom: Women's Human Rights in the Muslim World*, London/New York: I.B. Tauris.

Ahmed, L. (1992), *Women and Gender in Islam*, New Haven & London: Yale University Press.

Ardener, S. (1977), *Perceiving Women*, London: J.M. Dent.

Bateson, G. (1972), *Steps to an Ecology of Mind*, Toronto: Chandler Publishing Company.

Brink, J. and J. Mencher (eds) (1997), *Mixed Blessings: Gender and Religious Fundamentalism Cross Culturally*, New York and London: Routledge.

Brown, D. (1996), *Rethinking Tradition in Modern Islamic Thought*, Cambridge Middle East Studies: Cambridge University Press.

Gellner, E. (1992), *Postmodernism, Reason and Religion*, London: Routledge.

Hawley, J. Stratton (ed.) (1994), *Fundamentalism and Gender*. New York: Oxford University Press.

Kandioyoti, D. (1991), *Women, Islam and the State*, London: Macmillan.

de Lauretis, T. (1987), *The Technologies of Gender: Essays on Theory, Film and Fiction*, Bloomington: Indiana University Press.

Moore, H. (1994), *A Passion for Difference: Essays in Anthropology and Gender*, Cambridge: Cambridge Polity Press.

Roy, O. (1994), *The Failure of Political Islam*, London: I.B. Tauris.

Sagal, G. and N. Yuval Davies (1992), *Refusing Holy Orders*, London: Virago Press.

Taraki, L. (1996), 'Jordanian Islamist and the Agenda for Women: Between Discourse and Practice', *Middle Eastern Studies*, vol. 32, no. 1.

Torab, A. (1996), 'Piety as Gendered Agency: a Study of *Jalaseh* Ritual Discourse in an Urban Neighbourhood in Iran', *The Journal of the Royal Anthropological Institute,* vol. 2, no. 2.

Yamani, M. (ed.) (1996), *Feminism and Islam: Legal and Literary Perspectives*, London: Ithaca Press.

Chapter 1

Feminist Reinterpretation of Islamic Sources: Muslim Feminist Theology in the Light of the Christian Tradition of Feminist Thought

Anne Sofie Roald

Introduction

In the last decade there has been an increasing concern with women's rights in Islam. Not only have Muslim feminists highlighted the status of women in Muslim societies but Islamists,[1] male and female, have also joined the debate, stressing the liberating potential Islam has for women. During my fieldwork in Malaysia in 1991-2, I came across a group called 'Sisters in Islam'. It consisted mainly of highly educated Malay women, but also included some Western converts to Islam. They had an Islamic profile and they distributed pamphlets with titles such as 'Are Muslim men allowed to beat their wives?' In Karachi, Pakistan, in February 1992 I met a group of women at Karachi University with a very similar perspective. During my visit to Jordan in April 1992, I found that with regard to women's issues, female perspectives were mainly a matter for the more secularized forces in society. However, on revisiting Jordan in the summer of 1995 I was thrown directly into the debate on the Muslim woman's position in society. Interestingly, this debate was conducted in one of the headquarters of the Islamists in Jordan, in the Islamic Studies and Research Association (ISRA), also known as the Jordanian Centre for the International Institute of Islamic Thought (IIIT). Over a period of three years, Islamists' attitudes towards gender and gender relations had changed character. Muslim women's reinterpretation of Islamic sources is thus a matter of interest as it is not only an intellectual discussion within a feminist sphere but has entered the contemporary Islamist debate, as well.

This study will focus on the feminist intellectual discussion: what has been done in this respect and which subjects have been considered significant. Can a feminist reinterpretation of Islamic sources be set in the context of Islamic theology, i.e. is it possible that this trend might influence established Islamic theology? It is also of importance to examine the Muslim feminist tradition's relevance to a Christian feminist theology: what similarities exist and where do they divert?

The centennial anniversary of the publication of *The Woman's Bible* was observed in 1995. Elizabeth Cady Stanton was the main editor of this work and together with the black feminist Anna Julia Cooper's book, *A Voice from the South* (1892), it marked a turning point in Christian feminist theology. Early Arab feminists, such as the Lebanese Nazīra Zayn ad-Dīn, incorporated feminist ideas into an Islamic frame of reference. In 1928 she published a book called *Removing the Veil and Veiling*, which aroused the anger of Islamic scholars. It will be interesting to see whether Muslims will simply repeat the development of the Christian tradition or whether Islam is so inherently different from Christianity that a comparison between the two religions is impossible. This question can also be posed regarding matters such as whether Islam will be as secularized as Christianity, in the sense of a separation between church and state (*din wa dunya*). I suggest that the development of feminist ideas within an Islamic framework necessarily will end up asking such a question, but at the inauguration of a feminist reinterpretation of Islamic sources other matters are emphasized.

Reformation or Reconstruction

An important issue in the Christian and Judaic feminist tradition is whether the aim is *reformation* or *reconstruction*. On the one hand, feminists can regard the holy text as limited by its historical context and thus fragment it, classifying the fragments according to what is regarded as either universal and essential or culturally relative. On the other hand, feminists can regard the holy text as androcentric and manmade in the interest of men. The last position was that of Cady Stanton and the implication of this point of view is far-reaching.

Another issue which is closely related to the question of reform or reconstruction is whether interpretation of the holy text should be within a patriarchal framework or outside it. A reform would imply a degree of acceptance of existing ideas, whereas a reconstruction would imply a refutation of the same ideas. Within the tradition of feminist theological hermeneutics, Carolyn Osiek distinguishes between five hermeneutic approaches to the biblical text by contemporary feminists: *loyalist*, *revisionist*, *sublimationist*, *rejectionist*, and *liberationist*.

According to Osiek, the *loyalists* accept the Bible as divine revelation and the word of God but at the same time they claim the divine intention of man and woman living together in happiness and respect (Osiek 1985: 99). Turid Karlsen Seim,[2] a Norwegian researcher on the new testament, speaks of *fundamentalist woman's exegesis*, thus indicating a literal reading of the text, and this particular approach fits into Osiek's *loyalist* category. The *revisionists*, according to Osiek, believe that the patriarchal framework for the Judaeo-Christian tradition is historically and culturally but not theologically determined. The revisionist approach to reading the Bible involves a search for positive role models for women and an interpretation of the text from a feminist point of view. The *sublimationists* tend to read the Bible allegorically, presupposing equality of maleness and femaleness or even a preference for femininity (ibid.: 100, 102). She characterizes Cady Stanton among the *rejectionists*, stating that as regards the Bible as well as Christianity and Judaism, Cady Stanton considered them to be so permeated by patriarchal ideas that they had to be rejected. The fifth category, *liberationist* feminism, yearns for a transformation of the social order. The focus is on women's liberation in this world through a female struggle against all oppression (ibid.: 103). These five categories can be incorporated into the model of *reformation* and *reconstruction* where *loyalists*, *revisionists* and *sublimationists* can be classified as *reformers* whereas *rejectionists* and *liberationists* are *reconstructors*.

In the new Muslim feminist tradition several of these categories defined by Osiek are visible. Nawal el-Saadawi can be characterized as *rejectionist*, whereas from the writings of Amina Wadud-Muhsin and Riffat Hassan we can classify them both as *loyalist* and *revisionist*. Fatima Mernissi and Leila Ahmed are the closest to the *liberationist* scholarship. However, these categories are not totally distinguishable. Islam plays such a fundamental role in Muslim societies that for a social reformer to exclude Islam necessarily means failure. Many feminists, who previously struggled against female oppression in Western feminist terms have therefore now adopted a more favourable attitude towards Islam. For example, Fatima Mernissi in her study *Beyond the Veil* (first published in 1975) considered that changes in the conditions of women could be done without the framework of Islam, whereas in her book *Women and Islam* (first published in 1987) she has shifted attitude and believes that such a change has to be done from within Islam through a reinterpretation of Islamic sources. However, Mernissi does not give her point of view on the authority of the Koran in either of these two works. The work of Leila Ahmed points in the same direction, as she is vague in her attitude towards Islam. In her 1992 book *Women and Gender in Islam*, she expresses the view that Islam's coming brought with it a deterioration in the status of women in some places, whereas in other places it had a liberating effect. She does not, however, explicitly reject Islam, but rather the common interpretations of the Islamic sources. It seems that by focusing on Islam, the principles of female liberation have acquired a certain validity in Muslim society, as Islamically-minded women would sympathize with some of the arguments.

As for Wadud-Muhsin and Hassan, both tend to analyze the Koran within a framework accepted by many Islamic scholars. Although several of their arguments would be contested by these scholars, their works are part of an internal Islamic debate.

The Question of Authority

The question of authority is a vital one in both the Judaeo-Christian and Islamic debates. There are two levels of authority concerning the holy scriptures, the authority of *the text* and the authority of *the interpretation of the text*. Elisabeth Schüssler Fiorenza has noted that the feminist biblical discourses have been caught up in an apologetic debate which seeks to show that the

Bible, or at least parts of it, is *either* liberating and therefore has authority for women ... *or* that it is totally patriarchal and must be rejected (Schüssler Fiorenza 1994). This issue, which she labels 'the apologetic debate', is very much part of the new Muslim feminist debate although less explicit than in the Judaeo-Christian one which has gone on for more than a hundred years. As shown above, in most of her work Mernissi does not explicitly reject the Koran as the word of God, but neither does she explicitly accept it.

The concept of the holy text as the word of God has today different implications in Christianity and Islam. A common notion among researchers of Islam has been that the Koran is to Islam what Jesus is to Christianity. The development of the historical-critical method in the biblical debate has revealed that the question of whether the Bible contains words coming directly from God or whether it is only human narration about holy persons and happenings is not as fundamental as the question of whether the Koran is the word of God or not. It is possible to regard Jesus as 'the son of God' in spite of a degrading of the holy text, whereas Islam's theology is contingent on the belief that the Koran is the word of God (*kalām allāh*) which exists in heaven 'in a preserved tablet' (*fī lawhin mahfuz* [K. 85: 22]).

The question of authority related to the interpretation of the Islamic sources is emphasized in the debate. In Christianity, Schüssler Fiorenza has noted that the project of *The Woman's Bible* started 'with the realization that throughout the centuries the Bible has been invoked both as a weapon against and as a defence for subjugated women in their struggles for access to citizenship, public speaking, theological education, or ordained ministry' (Schüssler Fiorenza 1994: 5). This ambiguity of the holy text rests on differences of interpretation. As every interpreter has his or her own distinctive biography, this will influence the reading of the text. The interpreter's biography involves a person's specific character-traits, upbringing and experiences as well as class, status and gender (Hastrup 1992).

There is, however, another issue involved in Schüssler Fiorenza's expression. As theological deductions from the sacred texts have been a matter for elite males and thus favourable for men at the expense of female interests, religion has been the means for women to endure oppression. Schüssler Fiorenza has asserted that women's biblical heritage is 'at one and the same time a source for women's religious power and for women's suffering' (1994: 8).

An important question to pose is, *who has the authority to interpret the Islamic sources?* The traditional understanding in Islam has been that the interpreters of Islamic theology should be males only. Due partly to the gender-segregation in Muslim society with a traditional division of labour, where men are in charge of the civil life whereas women are supposed to keep to the domestic sphere, and partly to the low educational standard Muslim women used to have, the ideas of female Koranic interpreters have been refuted. There are records of female intellectuals and teachers in Muslim history (Berkey 1991: 143-75), but it is difficult to judge whether these women simply transmitted male knowledge or created knowledge of their own.

Female Perspectives

A probable hypothesis would be that when female perspectives come into focus the interpretations of the Islamic sources change. However, this is not always true. The first known woman to comment on the Koran was A'isha 'Abd ar-Rahmān (Bint ash-Shātī') born in 1913 in Egypt. She was a professor of Arabic literature in Cairo and a professor of Koranic studies in Morocco. According to Andrew Rippin, a researcher on Islam, A'isha 'Abd ar-Rahmān saw the Koranic aim to be spiritual and religious guidance, and not to give historical facts (Rippin 1993: 94). Although she emphasizes the importance of regarding the Koran according to time and place of revelation, her approach is not feminist. It is interesting to note that Schüssler Fiorenza (1994: 14) stresses that a woman who reads the Bible does not necessarily read it from a female perspective. She claims that 'to the contrary, women's writing and speaking often function to mediate and reinforce kyriarchal behaviour'. Schüssler Fiorenza further argues: 'One must also consider that women, even more than men, have internalized cultural-religious feminine values and that they consequently tend to reproduce uncritically the patriarchal politics of submission and otherness in their speaking and writing' (ibid.: 15).

As regards 'A'isha 'Abd ar-Rahmān, this observation seems plausible. Rippin has labelled her as 'neo-traditionalist' and states that her approach to the Koran is 'conservative' (Rippin 1993: 94). That is, although she is critical, her criticism is directed to the rigidity of earlier interpretations in general, rather than to traditional assumptions of femininity or womanhood.

It took a little more than thirty years from the publication of *The Woman's Bible* in 1895, to the first feminist interpretation of the Islamic sources. However, from this first step up to the 1970s and 1980s, Muslim feminists tended to regard the feminist case in purely Western terms and Islam was not brought into the debate. With the advent of the Islamic resurgence from the end of the sixties onwards, the Islamic issue came to the forefront even in the feminist debate. In a short time many Muslim women have published books and articles dealing with a reinterpretation of the Islamic sources. It is also interesting to note that in the 1980s two Islamic scholars, Muhammad al-Ghazzālī and Abd al-Halīm Abū Shaqqa, took up the subject of Muslim women. Their starting point is in the present situation of oppression in the Muslim world, claiming this to be a result of ignorance of 'the true Islam'. Their method is a reinterpretation of the *ahādīth* (Prophet Muhammad's sayings, actions and decisions (sing. *hadīth*) in two stages. Firstly, they take care to verify the authenticity of the *hadīth*, as they claim that many previously regarded as authentic (*sahīh*) in reality are either good (*hasan*), weak (*daī'f*), or forged.[3] The second step is to interpret the *ahādīth* in the light of the Koran. If the common interpretation is not compatible with the Koranic text, the *hadīth* if authentic, has to be reinterpreted in order to agree with the Koranic view. Abū Shaqqa in particular, claims that many widespread *ahādīth* talking about women in a negative way are forged. These scholars' efforts seem to be independent of the recent Muslim feminism. Rather, their works can be regarded as part of a dialogue with 'the West'. The massive attack by Western scholars on the position of women in Islam has opened up the issue for reinterpretations by well-known Islamic scholars. The issue of gender relations is sensitive in a Muslim context and it requires courage as well as a good reputation to raise such an issue. The reactions of other Islamic scholars have been harsh, but less harsh than those towards Muslim feminists.[4]

In 1982 *Women's Studies International Forum Magazine* dedicated an issue to the subject *Women and Islam.* Apart from contributions by researchers on Islam, Muslim feminists were also invited to come forward. Aziza al-Hibri wrote *A story of Islamic herstory: Or how did we ever get into this mess?,* which was influenced by the contemporary biblical feminist debate. Nawal el-Saadawi and Fatima Mernissi also contributed articles to the magazine, but their contributions are marked by a secular approach and they are more concerned with Muslim practice than with overarching theological questions. In 1985 Riffat Hassan brought up 'theological inquiries' into the Islamic sources. She emphasizes the equality of the sexes which can be read into the story of the creation in the Koran and compares this view with the *hadīth* literature where a totally opposite view on gender relations can be found. Fatima Mernissi published *Women and Islam* in 1987, drawing attention to the *ahādīth* on women in order to investigate their authenticity. She chooses to concentrate on the reliability of the narrators of these *ahādīth.* She argues that Abū Hurayra, a famous narrator of *ahādīth* was a misogynist, thus colouring the *ahādīth* he transmitted from the Prophet with his own views (Mernissi 1991: 62-81).

She also attacks the use of *hijāb* (the headscarf), claiming that there is no Koranic evidence that the wearing of a veil is an Islamic obligation. Refusal of the Islamic use of a veil is common among Muslim feminists. Leila Ahmed, in her book *Women and Gender in Islam*, argues that veiling for women was a requisite for the wives of the Prophet only (1992: 55). It is interesting to note that the idea of veiling as a symbol of oppression has been rejected by Samīra Fayyād, a leading Islamist who has been active in the struggle for female influences in the Islamist movement in Jordan. She argues as follows:

> There are many roots of this insignificance in women's position. The first of which is the divergence of women's liberation movements away from the essence of the problem. Those involved in the movement should have joined the mainstream of a general liberation movement working for the liberation of man and woman in times when both were suffering. Upholding her banner of women's liberation emphasized her peculiarities

as female and overlooked her integral nature as a rational and sensible human being. Rather she should have concerned herself with the national problems side by side along with men bearing full responsibility, ignoring marginal matters such as changing dress-styles and other trivialities (Fayyad 1992: 3).

The issue of the veil exposes fully the tension in the Muslim feminist debate between the *reformers* and the *reconstructors*. As the debate is in its inaugural phase the differences are to some extent concealed, whereas the tension will probably become more and more visible as the debate progresses.

The most common issues in the contemporary feminist reinterpretation of Islamic sources are:

(1) Re-evaluation of Islamic sources
(2) Criticism of the use of Islamic sources
(3) Criticism of interpretations of Islamic sources
(4) Equality of men and women in the Koran

I will exemplify these issues by referring to the two Muslim feminists, Amina Wadud-Muhsin and Riffat Hassan. As stated earlier, they can both be classified in the *loyalist* and *revisionist* approach identified by Carolyn Osiek. I have chosen to deal only with the *reform* feminists as there is a probability that ordinary Muslims and Islamists will take their views into account and thereby open a discussion with them. This has to a certain extent occurred, as Amina Wadud-Muhsin received the King Faysal Prize for her academic work *Qur'an and Woman* in 1994. The reputation of Fatima Mernissi and Nawal el-Saadawi in Muslim society is that of 'Western feminists' and very few Muslims outside the ranks of Muslim feminists would find their writings relevant.

Re-evaluation of Islamic Sources

Amina Wadud-Muhsin has in her work been concerned with the study of the Koran only. She has not taken *ahādīth*, into consideration. Hassan, on the other hand, devotes a great part of her study to *ahādīth*, although she states that she will concentrate on the Koran as it is '*the* primary source of *normative* Islam'

(1990: 93). She explains *ahādīth* to be 'the lens through which the words of the Koran have been seen and interpreted' (ibid.: 94). She takes her starting point in a discussion of 'the Islamic tradition', which she considers to be the Islamic texts (Koran and *ahādīth*) as well as the whole body of regulations and laws built on these texts. She refers to the refutations of *ahādīth* by what she calls 'moderate' Muslims — such as the Pakistani intellectual Ghulam Ahmad Parwez and the Indian scholar Moulvi Cheragh Ali — and to the quotations of famous Orientalist scholars — such as Alfred Guillaume and H.A.R. Gibb — where they invalidate the *hadīth* literature. Thus she manages to raise doubts about the validity of *ahādīth*. Although she believes that one has to be sceptical towards the *hadīth* literature, she recognizes that to a certain extent the *ahādīth* are necessary and agrees with Fazlur Rahman that, 'If the *hadīth* literature as a whole is cast away, the basis for the historicity of the Koran is removed with one stroke' (ibid.: 94).

Criticism of the Use of Islamic Sources

Both Amina Wadud-Muhsin's and Riffat Hassan's approach to the study of the Koran is in the first place hermeneutical. Wadud-Muhsin explains her hermeneutical model as being concerned with firstly, the context in which the Koranic passages were written, secondly, the grammatical composition of these passages and thirdly, the world-view of the Koran. As for the latter she states that most of the former Koran commentators would have an atomistic methodology, as they would interpret one verse at a time without regarding the text as one part of a whole (Wadud-Muhsin 1992: 2).

Hassan claims that religion is being used as an instrument of oppression rather than as a means of liberation' (Hassan 1990: 96). She further argues that 'the negative attitudes pertaining to women which prevail in Muslim societies, in general, are rooted in theology'. She believes that Muslims in general 'consider it a self-evident truth that women are not equal to men' (ibid.: 100), a belief which in Hassan's view lies in three theological assumptions:

(1)   that God's primary creation is man, not woman, since woman is believed to have been created from man's rib, hence is derivative and ontologically secondary;

(2)   that woman, not man, was the primary agent of what is customarily described as 'Man's Fall' or Man's expulsion from the garden of Eden, hence 'all daughters of Eve' are to be regarded with hatred, suspicion and contempt; and

(3)   that woman was created not only *from* man, but also *for* man, which makes her existence merely instrumental and not of fundamental importance (ibid.: 100-1).

Hassan gives three main explanations of these theological assumptions. Firstly, the patriarchal environment in Muslim society has made Islamic scholars during history interpret Islamic sources in terms of male hegemony. Secondly, many *ahādīth* with negative attitudes towards women are in circulation in Muslim society although their authenticity has been questioned and their popularity, even among Islamic scholars, points to the view of women as subordinate to men, as being deeply embedded in Muslim society (ibid.: 103). In presenting her arguments, Hassan also indicates that many *ahādīth* about women are forged as she believes that there are incompatibilities between passages in the Koran and many of these *ahādīth*. She even criticizes the position of the *hadīth* collections by al-Bukhārī (1984) and Muslim (1971) in Islamic jurisprudence, believing that Muslims accept the two collections as being on a like footing with the Koran.

To Islamic scholars, Islamists' and even common Muslims' criticism of the *ahādīth* might be regarded as criticism against Islam itself. This makes the project of a feminist reading of the Islamic sources a very delicate matter as there exist utterances related to the Prophet which convey negative views of women — such as, for instance, that the majority of the inhabitants of Hell are women (Muslim 1971: 1431 (vol. IV)). Some feminists would refute these sayings, claiming them as forgeries, whereas others, such as Wadud-Muhsin have chosen to leave out the matter of *ahādīth* and concentrate solely on the Koranic text and its previous interpreters. However, this method is problematic as the *ahādīth* are regarded as the explanation of the Koran and thus have strong authority in Islamic theology. Others again, such as the Islamist Samīra Fayyād, together with male Islamists, such as Muhammad al-Ghazzālī and 'Abd al-Halīm Abū Shaqqa, would explain these hermeneutically, emphasizing the specific situation of every *hadīth*. Thus this specific *hadīth* mentioned above would be explained as an admonition made by the Prophet to women in general and should be understood as a general reminder (*tadkira*) (Abu Shaqqa 1990: 273).

The differences in interpretations and understandings of *ahādīth* point to the multivalence of the text. Not only will *ahādīth* be interpreted differently in different contexts, but it also depends on the interpreter how the text will be perceived. The subject of the researcher is also decisive for the understanding of the text. For example, a researcher on gender relations in Islam will search for statements about women only and might fail to notice that there are expressions about men and human beings in the Islamic sources which convey negative views of both men as a category and humankind as a whole. However, these statements have not been understood as generalizations by Muslims themselves, but rather as admonitions and reminders that human beings should follow the path of God. On the other hand, as even Islamist scholars have noticed, many *ahādīth* have actually been interpreted in terms of male preference or have been presented as authentic (*sahīh*) although they are either only good (*hasan*) or weak (*da'īf*) (Shaqqa 1990; al-Ghazzali 1989 and 1991; al-Qardāwī 1990).

Criticism of Interpretations of the Islamic Sources

The traditional interpretation of Islamic sources is high on the agenda of the modern feminist debate. Wadud-Muhsin (1992: 2) discusses the objectivity of the interpreters of the Koran, claiming that not one of them can be wholly objective as their 'subjective choices' would colour the result of their research. Her main criticism is not of the commentators, but rather of the common conception that there is no distinction between text and interpretation; thus there is a tendency to elevate interpretations to a holy level. She characterizes three approaches to the interpretations of women in the Koran: 'traditional', 'reactive', and 'holistic'. The 'traditional' exegetical works (*tafāsīr* sing. *tafsīr*) she explains as those which interpret the entire Koran with certain objectives in mind, such as grammar, esotericism, rhetoric, history, or legislation. She claims this approach to be atomistic with no underlying hermeneutical principles in order to interpret each part of the Koran in the light of the Koran as a whole. In addition, all of these interpretations, both from classical and modern times, have been written by men, and Wadud-Muhsin thus believes that women's experiences have been either excluded from the text or 'interpreted through male vision, perspective, desire, or needs of women' (1992: 2).

The 'reactive' approach to the interpretation of the Koran has, according to Wadud-Muhsin, mainly been concerned with criticism of the Koran and Islam. Modern scholars have justified this criticism because of the poor status of women in Muslim society. However, Wadud-Muhsin states that these scholars, likewise, do not distinguish between the text and the interpreter.

The aim of Wadud-Muhsin's study is to demonstrate the best tool for the liberation of Muslim women, namely to turn to the Koran, 'the primary source of Islamic ideology and theology' (ibid.: 2-3). This represents the third approach, the 'holistic' interpretation of the Koran. According to her, this method includes modern social, moral, economic, and political aspects and even the issue of women. She refers to Fazlur Rahman's principle of interpreting Koranic passages, saying:

> He [Fazlur Rahman] suggests that all Koranic passages, revealed as they were in a specific time in history and within certain general and particular circumstances, were given expression relative to those circumstances. However, the message is not limited to that time or those circumstances historically. A reader must understand the implications of the Koranic expressions during the time in which they were expressed in order to determine their proper meaning. That meaning gives the intention of the rulings or principles in the particular verse (ibid.: 4).

The project of reinterpretation or of turning back to the primary sources without regarding previous scholarship as infallible, started with the intellectual *salafiyya* movement in the nineteenth century. Although women's issues were not particularly emphasized, some reforms in the view of women were visible. One example is Muhammad Abduh's interpretation of the verse of polygamy in the Koran. Turning away from the common understanding that marrying more than one woman is well accepted, if not obligatory, he suggested that the last part of the verse should take effect, namely: 'But if you fear that you might not be able to treat them [the wives] with equal fairness, then [marry only] one ... This will make it more likely that you will not deviate from the right course' (K. 4: 3).

In Western society feminist thought achieved a breakthrough in the sixties and seventies and brought with it a kind of relativism, as perspectives changed. It became obvious that 'the objectivity' of the researcher was only an illusion. Various sciences opened up for new interpretations as it became clear that previous research results had been dominated by male perspectives. The reinterpretation of the Islamic sources by women is a new project and the next decades will show us whether this project has any future. Let us now turn to the reinterpretation in order to examine the elements involved.

Equality of Men and Women in the Koran

Initially in the Muslim feminist theological debate the idea of equality between the sexes in the Koran is emphasized. This study is mainly concerned with the ideological level and will thus take up the question how gender relations have been perceived anthropologically and cosmologically. I will concentrate on two main issues: How is the creation of human being in the Koran interpreted by the feminists? And how do they perceive the role of women on earth?

Creation of Human Being

Wadud-Muhsin asks the questions 'Do the Koranic accounts of the process of the creation of humankind distinguish woman from man in such a way as to confine her potential to a single biologically determined role? Does it imply created inferiority?' (Wadud-Mahsin 1992: 15-16)

She argues that although the Koran distinguishes between man and woman she finds no differences in value between them. It is, however, important to notice that Islamic scholars in various times have accentuated the very same point, but they have tended to link this equality to the relationship between man and the Creator only. Thus, equality of man and woman for both *madhhabists*[5] and the more modern Islamists signifies religious equality, i.e. equality in Islamic obligations, such as praying and fasting; whereas sociologically man and woman are depicted as having different roles. This division of roles related to gender contrasts with the Western paradigm where social equality rests in the first place on economic equality: whether women have either private economic means or property or take active part in the production of society.

Wadud-Muhsin has attacked the common understanding of gender relations in Islam. She bases her arguments concerning equality between men and women in the Koran on human being's incomprehension of the supernatural. To make these matters understandable for mankind, according to her, they need to be rendered in human language. Thus, in the Koran we can find references to other worldly happenings which we as human beings must interpret allegorically (ibid.: 15-6). Wadud-Muhsin turns to the story of creation in the Koran. She believes that attitudes towards women in Muslim society are built on the interpretation of this story. She takes her starting point in the Koranic verse:

> And from (*min*) His signs (*ayāt*) is that He created you (humankind) from (*min*) a single soul (*nafs*), and created from (*min*) it its mate (*zawj*), and from (*min*) these two He spread countless men and women (K. 4: 1)

From this verse she extracts key terms, such as *min, nafs* and *zawj*. As for *min* she claims that it can be used for the preposition *from* in the meaning of *extracting things from other things*. It can also, according to Wadud-Muhsin, be used to imply 'of the same nature as' and she states that in the Koranic verse above the meaning changes according to which translation of the preposition one chooses. She refers to al-Zamakhsharī (d.1144 CE), a famous commentator on the Koran, saying that he interprets this verse as meaning that 'humankind was created *in/of the same type as* a single *nafs,* and that the *zawj* of that *nafs* was taken *from* that *nafs*'. She says that he has found backing for his argumentation in biblical versions (ibid.: 18).

It is important to be aware of that most of the commentators of the Koran from the first centuries of Islamic history onwards incorporated many Jewish interpretations or Talmudic accounts of

various biblical stories (*isrā'īliyāt*) which have their counterparts
in the Koran. In the modern Islamist debate, however, many of
these stories have been weeded from these *tafāsīr*. One example
is the famous *tafsīr* by Imād ad-Dī Ibn Kathīr (d.1372 CE), which
in the 1970s was examined by Shaykh Muhammad 'Alī as-Sābūnī.
The result was presented as *mukhtasar tafsīr Ibn Kathīr*
(Shortened Commentary by Ibn Kathīr) and it is regarded as
containing only authentic material.

With this in mind we have to turn back to Wadud-Muhsin's
discussion on the preposition *min* and how the Koranic verse
changes its meaning according to which understanding of *min* is
used. She states implicitly that al-Zamakhshārī arrived at his
conclusion wrongly as he depended on biblical material. However,
I would argue that al-Zamakhshārī's conclusion is not based on
these biblical materials which are classified as *isrā'īliyāt*; rather
it is a result of the understanding of a *hadīth* found in the *hadīth*
collections of both al-Bukhārī and Muslim related by Abū
Hurayra and thus accepted as authentic by orthodox Islam:

> Treat women kindly. The woman has been created from a rib, and the
> most crooked part of the rib is in the upper region. If you try to make it
> straight, you will break it, and if you leave it as it is, it will remain
> curved. So treat women kindly (Al-Bukhari 1984: 346 (vol. 4); Muslim
> 1971: 752 (vol. 2)).

Wadud-Muhsin actually mentions this *hadīth* in a footnote, saying
that according to Riffat Hassan the *hadīth,* although authentic,
belongs to the category of *hadīth āhād* which means that this
hadīth was reported by one person only (1992: 18-20). Hassan has
rejected not only the authority of chain of narrators (*isnād*), as
nobody other than Abū Hurayra has related this *hadīth,* but also
the text (*matn*) of the hadīth (K. 1990: 102). Both Hassan and
Wadud-Muhsin reject the *hadīth* as normative.

Hassan also emphasizes that 'God's original creation was
undifferentiated humanity and not either man and women' (ibid.:
102). She proves this by pointing to the meaning of 'Adam' in
Hebrew which is 'of the soil'. She further says that the Hebrew
term 'Adam' refers to 'the human' (species) rather than to a male
human being and in the Koran the term is used, in twenty-one
cases out of twenty-five, to refer to humanity. Also she states that

the Koran uses both feminine and masculine terms and imagery to describe the creation of humanity from a single source. In addition, the creation of Eve (Arabic: *Hawwā'*) from Adam's rib is never mentioned in the Koran, and even in the *hadīth* referred to above, Adam is not named. Hassan interprets the function of this *hadīth* to be 'further dehumanization' for women since the female species could - in the *ahādīth* in question - have been created from a disembodied rib which may not even have been human' (Hassan 1990: 127 footnote). It is interesting to note that a minority of Islamic scholars, such as Muhammad al-Ghazzālī, are of the view that *hadīth āhād* should not be normative either in legislation or in doctrine. There is thus a controversy between orthodox Islamic scholars which substantiates Wadud-Muhsin's criticism of al-Zamakhsharī's analysis of the Koranic verse above.

The next key term to be dealt with is *nafs*. Wadud-Muhsin observes that grammatically, *nafs* is feminine, whereas conceptually it is neither masculine nor feminine as according to her, the Koran never states that the creation of humankind started with the *nafs* of Adam. Thus she considers that the Koran does not express the creation of humankind in terms of gender (Wadud-Muhsin 1992: 20).

Both Hassan and Wadud-Muhsin have dealt with the key term *zawj*. Wadud-Muhsin stresses that *zawj* is masculine, grammatically speaking, whereas conceptually it is neither masculine nor feminine. Hassan goes further, saying that whereas the Koranic usage of *azwāj* refers to the married couple; man and woman, another form for 'couple', namely *zawjayn* (dual form of *zawj*), describes the process of ongoing creation, referring to the Koranic verses:

(1) 'And it is He who has created the two kinds (*zawjayn*), male and female out of a drop of sperm as it is poured forth' (K. 53: 45-6).

(2) 'Does human being, then, think, that he is left without a purpose? Was he not once a drop of sperm emitted? Then he did become a leech whereupon He created and formed [him] in due proportion. And he made out of him two sexes (*zawjayn*); male and female' (K. 75: 36-9).

She concludes from this that man and woman are 'two sexually-differentiated human beings - created by God from a unitary source *(nafsin wāhidatin)'*. Man and woman are therefore, according to Hassan, 'related to each other ontologically, not merely sociologically' (Hassan 1990: 89).

As for the common notion of women as temptresses prevailing in the Judaeo-Christian world as well as among Muslims, Wadud-Muhsin rejects the notion that this should be part of Islamic theology. She states that the Koran uses the dual form, with one exception, to tell how Satan tempted Adam and his mate *(zawj)* and how both disobeyed God. The one exception shows how *Adam* was tempted by Satan, and then the two of them (Adam and his mate) ate of the forbidden tree (Wadud-Muhsin 1992: 25).

According to Wadud-Muhsin and Hassan the creation of humankind is thus gender-neutral and nothing in the Koran or in reliable *ahādīth* points to the male gender as morally or intellectually superior to the female. Male and female as types are thus equal before God, with the same religious obligations and the same religious rights. This view does not differ from the view of most contemporary Islamists, who would explain men and women to have equal value but with different social tasks and obligations. There has been a modification of the view of women. This can be considered as a reaction against both modernism and modernity, where modernism depicts modern thought whereas modernity characterizes the technification of life (Lawrence 1989). These modifications can be observed in the works of the Islamic scholars Abū Shaqqa and al-Ghazzālī. However, among *madhhabists*, particularly in the circles of *ahl al-hadīth* (those who adhere to the *ahādīth*), and among the *salafīs*,[6] males are considered as possessing a higher value than females due to state-ments in various *ahādīth*, among them the *hadīth* referred to above.

It is of interest to turn to Christian feminist theologians and their interpretation of the act of creation in the Bible. Phyllis Bird is one of those who have dealt with this subject. She compares the two versions in Genesis, the Priestly account and the Yahwistic account. She states that the two stories contain no statement of dominance or subordination in the relationship of the sexes (Bird 1991: 20). She further argues that in the accounts:

> The social metaphors to which the key verbs point are male, derived from male experience and models, the dominant social models of patriarchal

society. For P, as for J, the representative and determining image of the species was certainly male ... Though the Priestly writer speaks of the species, he thinks of the male, just as the author of Psalm 8. But maleness is not an essential or defining characteristic (ibid.: 18).

It is important to note that although there is a similarity between Bird and Wadud-Muhsin in the perspective of gender-neutrality in creation of man in the two religions, Bird's historical-critical method leads her to draw conclusions, such as that the Bible was written by humans, an assumption which is not possible in an Islamic exegesis.

Roles of Women

When it comes to divisions of roles in Islam, Muslim feminists would part also from the common view of moderate Islamists. Wadud-Muhsin chooses to discuss the role of women from two perspectives:

(1)   There is no inherent value placed on man or woman. In fact, there is no arbitrary, preordained and eternal system of hierarchy.

(2)   The Koran does not strictly delineate the roles of woman and the roles of man to such an extent as to propose only a single possibility for each gender (that is, women must fulfil this role, and *only* this one, while men must fulfil that role and only men *can* fulfil it) (Wadud-Muhsin 1992: 63).

She claims that the Koran 'acknowledges that we operate in social systems with certain functional distinctions' (ibid.: 64). Further, Wadud-Muhsin sees that these functional distinctions included in the Koran have been used to support the idea of 'inherent superiority of men over women'. She asks two main questions: 'Are there certain exceptions and exclusions for males or females? Does the Koran value certain functions above others?'

Wadud-Muhsin observes that in the Koran the woman's primary *distinction* is on the basis of her childbearing ability. Thus, Muslims have regarded this ability as her primary function. However, she rejects this notion, claiming that there is no term in the Koran which indicates that childbearing is 'primary' to a woman and that 'no indication is given that mothering is her exclusive role' (ibid.: 64). In addition she rejects the notion that men are special because only men have been selected to be prophets. She points out that although there are no Koranic examples of female prophecies, women such as Maryam and the mother of Moses received revelations (*wāhy*) (ibid.: 65). In her opinion, all those chosen as prophets were exceptional human beings and the prophecy is thus not a specific characterization for males.

Wadud-Muhsin has analyzed two Koranic terms, *daraja* (step, degree of level) and *faddala* (to prefer) which 'have been used to indicate value in the functional distinctions between individuals and groups on earth' (ibid.: 66). She argues that the Koran 'does not divide the labour and establish a monolithic order for every social system which completely disregards the natural variations in society. On the contrary, it acknowledges the need for variations when it states that 'the human race is divided into nations and tribes that you might know one another' (K. 49: 13).' She thus concludes that the Koran allows and encourages each individual social context to determine its functional distinctions between members, but applies a single system of equitable recompense which can be adopted in every social context (Wadud-Muhsin 1992: 67).

She analyses the concept *daraja* in this perspective, saying that *daraja* is most often linked to doing 'good' deeds (ibid.: 66). God also gives *daraja* to individuals; either on the basis of knowledge (K. 58: 11) or on the basis of social or economic distinctions (K. 43: 32). Wadud-Muhsin quotes the Koranic statement: 'Unto men a fortune from that which they have earned, and unto women a fortune from that which they have earned' (K. 4: 32). From this discussion she turns to the verse in the Koran where men are said to be a *daraja* above women. Although this verse is specifically about divorce, she says Muslims have taken it to mean that a *daraja* exists between all men and women, in every context (Wadud-Muhsin 1992: 68). She believes that the advantage men have over women is that of 'being individually able to pronounce divorce against their wives without arbitration or assistance', whereas women can obtain a divorce only after the intervention of an authority (ibid.: 68). This interpretation, although plausible, seems to be limited. Wadud-Muhsin does not question the

common notion that a Muslim man can divorce his wife without
any intervention. The Koran does not give a specific procedure for
how to divorce and a more profound investigation of this matter
should be of interest in a study of the Koran and women.

Wadud-Muhsin turns to the term *faddala* (*faddala* means 'to
prefer' and *fadl* means 'preference'), and refers to three
'preferences' in the Koran: Firstly, humankind is preferred to the
rest of creation (K. 17: 70); secondly, occasionally one group of
people have been preferred to another (K. 2: 47, K. 2: 122, K. 7:
40); and thirdly, some of the prophets are preferred to others (K.
2: 253, K. 6: 86, K. 17: 55). She believes that preference is not
absolute, as although some prophets are preferred to others, there
is *no distinction* between them. Thus, she concludes that in
Koranic usage, 'preference is relative' (Wadud-Muhsin 1992: 69).
She notes that both *daraja* and *fadl* are given as tests, but unlike
daraja, faddala cannot be earned. *Fadl* is given by God to whom
he wants. As for *fadl* the central verse in the Koran is:

> Men are [*qawwāmūn 'alā*] women, [*bi*-on the basis] of what Allah has
> [*faddala* -preferred] some of them over others, and [*bi*-on the basis] of
> what they spend of their property (for the support of women) (K. 4: 34).

In her analysis, Wadud-Muhsin sees this in a material context,
saying that there is only one place in the Koran where men have
preference over women and that is in inheritance where men
inherit twice as much as women. She links this preference to the
obligation to spend of their property, which follows directly in the
verse, and concludes that 'there is a reciprocity between
privileges and responsibilities'(ibid.: 70-1). She says that 'men
have responsibility of paying out of their wealth for the support
of women, and they are consequently granted a double share of
inheritance'. Wadud-Muhsin rejects the notion that men were
created by God superior to women (in strength and reason), a
common interpretation of this verse. She believes that *faddala* is
not conditional as the text does not say that *they* (men) are
preferred to them (women). Rather it states that *some* of them are
over *some*. She asserts:

> The use of *ba'd* (some) relates to what obviously has been observed in
> the human context. All men do not excel over all women in all manners.

Some men excel over some women in some manners. Likewise, some women excel over some men in some manners. So, whatever Allah has preferred, it is still not absolute (ibid.: 71).

Wadud-Muhsin further discusses earlier interpretations of the expression *qawwāmūn 'alā*. She notes that Pickthall, an English convert to Islam who translated the Koran in the early twentieth century, perceives this expression as 'in charge of', and al-Zamakhsharī translates it as 'men are in charge of the affairs of women'. As for Mawdūdī, the Pakistani Islamist, he perceives the Koranic passage as 'men are the managers of the affairs of women because Allah has made the one superior to the other' (ibid.: 71). Lastly, she turns to Sayyid Qutb who regards this verse in a family context. Wadud-Muhsin also observes that Qutb believes that as men provide for their families, this gives the males the privilege to be *qawwāmūn 'alā* the females. However, he states that 'the man and the woman are both from Allah's creation and Allah ... never intends to oppress anyone from His creation' (ibid.: 73 quoted from Qutb 1980: 650 (vol. III)).

Building upon his argumentation, Wadud-Muhsin concludes that within the family each member has certain responsibilities. Ideologically speaking, women's primary responsibility is childbearing (human existence depends upon it), whereas men's responsibility is the support of the family (the continuation of the human race depends upon it). However, in contrast to this ideal Wadud-Muhsin says:

This ideal scenario establishes an equitable and mutually dependent relationship. However, it does not allow for many of today's realities. What happens in societies experiencing a population overload, such as China and India? What happens in capitalistic societies like America, where a single income is no longer sufficient to maintain a reasonably comfortable lifestyle? ... What happens to the balance of responsibility when the man cannot provide materially, as was often the case during slavery and post slavery US (ibid.: 73)?

Her view is that the Koran must eternally be reviewed and reinterpreted according to social conditions with stress on mutual responsibility between males and females. She further calls for a broadening of the concept *qiwāma* (guardianship) from the material sphere to include spiritual, moral, intellectual, and psychological dimensions as well. The Koranic passage 4: 34 has its counterpart in the Bible. Genesis 3: 16 states 'he shall rule over her' where rule is a translation of the verb *mashāl*. *Mashāl* can also be translated as manage or control and the resemblance to the Koranic term *qawwāmūn 'alā* is apparent. Bird (1991: 21) states:

> For the relationship of companionship, established in the creation and exhibited in the mutual drive of the sexes towards each other ... is broken by the added word of judgement: 'he shall rule over her' (3: 16). The companion of chapter 2 has become a master. The historical subordination of woman to man is inaugurated - and identified as the paradigm expression of sin and alienation in creation.

Reflections

Wadud-Muhsin and Hassan discuss matters which are also treated by the moderate Islamic scholars, such as the position of the *hadīth* literature in Islamic jurisprudence (*fiqh*) and the role of women in Islam. Hassan's discussion of the authority of *ahādīth* reveals her ambivalent attitude. Wadud-Muhsin does not explicitly reject the authority of *ahādīth,* but as she does not use them in her analysis of the Koran this implies that she does not fully support them either. The feminists take a stand *against* much of the *ahādīth* dealing with women in a negative way, whereas the Islamic scholars would not reject these *ahādīth* but would interpret them in a more favourable way. The discrepancy in view opens up a conflict as a re-evaluation of *ahādīth* is not generally accepted in Islamic theology. The reform feminists are obviously aware of this fact and that explains the vagueness in their formulations. They will thereby have an advantage, as their work might get a Muslim audience, whereas the reconstructors, such as Fatima Mernissi, Leila Ahmed and Nawal el-Saadawi, who are more outspoken in their criticism, would be read favourably by certain groups only.

In the view of women at the ideological level, Muslim reform feminism does not divert too much from moderate. For instance, the ideas of the widespread Islamic movement the Muslim Brotherhood on women are that men and women are equal in regard to divine worship, whereas they have different roles in society. However, in practice it seems that in the world-view of the Brothers 'social inequality' has eclipsed 'spiritual equality'. This is also true for the actually existing Muslim societies as women have a rather low social status estimated in economic terms. It is, however, important to pose the question whether a sociological model constructed in Western society is applicable to Muslim society as the economic and socio-political conditions are different. As mentioned above — Islamism and in particular moderate Islamism — is very much a modern phenomenon with modern perspectives. The same is true of Muslim countries which are mainly modern, secular states. It is therefore possible that many attitudes and values common in Western society can be found in Muslim society, too. Thus, the evaluation of women in Muslim society might be in accordance with global standards even by Muslims themselves. The view of Muslim women is therefore ambivalent: at the same time traditional and modern. Wadud-Muhsin's and Hassan's studies are in this context important as they try to adjust a modern view of women in Islam to a modern reality.

There is a distinction between Wadud-Muhsin and Hassan and the Christian feminist theologians which I have referred to above. The historical-critical methods used by Schüssler Fiorenza and Bird are part of an established scientific tradition within Christian theology. They do turn to the study of gender relations, which is a controversial issue within the same tradition, but they do not part too much from the established research tradition. In Islam the established research tradition is totally different. With the breakdown of the authority of the traditional *madhhab* (law-school system), the research concentrates mainly on textual analysis and thus works methodologically in search of evidences to establish laws and regulations suitable for modern society. Wadud-Muhsin and Hassan keep to the same research method.

Schüssler Fiorenza is basically text-oriented, i.e. she goes behind the text, reconstructing a historical action which she states does not have to be verified as historical fact. She is thus a *reconstructor* in the Christian feminist tradition. Likewise, Bird is a reconstructor as she deconstructs the text and regards it in its historical context. She believes that:

the revelatory content of the word [the biblical text] and its contemporary meaning are apprehended only through this conversation [which has both ancient (canonical and post-canonical) and contemporary partners] and may not be identified with any particular text or locution nor with the author's imputed intention (Bird 1991: 24).

Wadud-Muhsin and Hassan on the other hand, are interpretation-oriented, i.e. they make semantic analysis in order to change common interpretations of the text and are thus *reformers* in the Islamic tradition. However, in spite of the obvious differences in approach of Schüssler Fiorenza and Wadud-Muhsin and Hassan, I would suggest that their positions within their respective traditions are similar. There is a discrepancy between Christianity and Islam, particularly in the literal reading of the text, which appears most clearly in a comparison between the story of creation in the Bible and in the Koran, as in the Koran Eve is neither depicted as a temptress nor created by the rib of Adam. Wadud-Muhsin (1992: vi) explains:

In other religions, feminists have had to insert woman into the discourse [of the interpretations of the holy texts] in order to attain legitimacy. The Muslim woman has only to read the text - unconstrained by exclusive and restrictive interpretations - to gain an undeniable liberation.

In this context it is also important to note that feminist Christian reconstructors perceive the Bible as written by human beings and in particular by men, whereas Muslim feminist reformers most probably would perceive the Koran as the 'Word of God'. There do exist feminist Christian fundamentalists who would also regard the Bible as the 'Word of God', but I consider this group to be less similar to Islamic feminists both in aims and in methodology than are the feminist Christian reconstructors.

Among the *loyalist* categorization by Osiek, there are the feminists belonging to the evangelical tradition of an exegesis of the Bible. This approach can be comparable to that of the Muslim feminists discussed above. Likewise with the starting point of Wadud-Muhsin, this tradition requires a view of the revealed text as an absolute authority. Is it thus possible to place Wadud-Muhsin and Hassan in a fundamentalist[7] tradition as expressed by Karlsen Seim? The answer would be *yes* if fundamentalism stands

for a 'return to the pure sources of Islam' and it would be *no* if
it stands for a political interpretation of Islam (Haddad 1987: 234-
59 and Roald 1994 for further discussion on fundamentalist
terminology). It is, though, important to be aware of the
distinction between fundamentalism in a Christian sense of the
word and in its Islamic context. The former indicates a literal
interpretation of the text whereas the latter is explained above as
meaning 'a return to the pure sources', thus going beyond the
development of Islamic theology. However, Islamic does not
necessarily imply a literal reading of the Koran and the *ahādith*.
The similarity between feminist theology in Christianity and Islam
can appear amazing as there is a common notion of the two
religious spheres as being far apart. However, by turning on the
one hand to the background of a joint Middle Eastern heritage as
a starting point for a common framework of social and spiritual
ideas, and on the other hand to the common problematic of the
contemporary Global Village, differences seem rather minor,
depending on developments in different times and places, rather
than as fundamental and absolute.

Notes

1. I use the term 'Islamism' and avoid using 'Islamic
    fundamentalism' as fundamentalism denotes a Christian
    direction with a literary reading of the Bible. Islamism does
    not imply a literary reading of the Islamic sources, rather it
    promotes the idea of regarding Islam as 'a complete system',
    a body of ideas, values, beliefs and practices encompassing
    all spheres of life (cf. Haddad 1987; Roald 1994).
2. Discussion with Turid Karlsen Seim, 16 February 1995.
3. In science of *hadīth* these three categories *sahīh, hasan* and
    da'īf relate to the authenticity of the chain of narrators
    (*isnād*) and to the text (*matn*) of the *hadīth*.
4. Amina Wadud-Muhsin went to South Africa and during her
    stay there she gave a lecture in one of the mosques. The
    reaction of the *ulamā* was hard. In one of the periodicals, *The
    Majlis: Voice of Islam*, she was attacked and one of the state-
    ments was: 'Anyone who claims to be a Muslim and then
    supports any satanic scheme of reinterpreting the Koran or
    the *shar'īa* leaves the fold of Islam. He is a *murtadd*

(apostate)' *(The Majlis: Voice of Islam* 1994: 5 (vol. 11 no. 7).
5. cf. Roald 1994: 17. I define *madhhabist* as those Muslims who adhere to the *madhhabs* (the four law-schools).
6. The Salafi Movement is a movement which has strengthened its position in the Arab world from the seventies onwards. It is marked by a strict adherence to the *ahādīth* and a total rejection of the *madhhabi* system. For further information see Roald 1994.
7. Arab Muslims use the Arabic term *usūl*. However, this term has, in contrast to the English 'fundamentalist', a positive connotation and denotes a person who searches back to the proper legal evidences (*al-ahkām ash-shara'iyya*) of the sources of Islam.

References

Abū Shaqqa, Abd al-Halīm (1990), *tahrīr al-mara a fī asr ar-risāla*, (Dār al-qalam li n-nashr wat-tawzī) Kuwait.

Ahmed, L. (1992), *Women and Gender in Islam*, New Haven: Yale University Press.

Berkey, J.P. (1991), 'Women and Islamic Education in the Mamluk Period' in N. Keddie and B. Baron (eds) *Women in Middle Eastern History*, New Haven: Yale University Press.

Bird, P.A. (1991), 'Sexual Differentiation and Divine Image in the Genesis Creation Texts', *Image of God and Gender Models*, Oslo: Solum forlag.

al-Bukhāri (1984), *Sahih al-Bukhāri*, New Dehli: Kitab Bhavan.

Fayyād, S. (1992), 'Future opportunities and prospects for women in Islam,' From a paper submitted to a seminar on Muslim-Christian dialogue at the Vatican in Rome, June.

al-Ghazzāli, M. (1989), *as-sunna an-nabawiyya bayna ahl al-fiqh wa ahl al-adth,* Cairo: Dār ash-Shurūq.

al-Ghazzāli, M. (1991), *kayfa nata'āmal ma' al-qurān*, Herndon: International Institute for Islamic Thought.

Haddad, Y.Y. (1987), 'Islamic Awakening in Egypt', *Arab Studies Quarterly* vol. 9, no. 3.

Hassan, R. (1990), 'An Islamic Perspective', in J. Becher (ed.), *Women, Religion and Sexuality*, Geneva Kitab Bhavan World Council of Churches Publications.

Hastrup, K. (1992), 'Writing Ethnography: State of Art', in J. Okely & H. Callaway (eds), *Anthropology and Autobiography*, London: Routledge.

Ibn Kathir Imād ad-Din (1973), *mukhtasar tafsīr ibn Kathīr* (vols. I-III), Beirut: Dār al-Qurān al-Karim 4.

Lawrence, B. (1989), *The Defenders of God: The Fundamentalist Revolt against the Modern Age,* London: I.B. Taurus & Co.

The Majlis: Voice of Islam (1994), vol. 11, no. 7.

Mernissi, F. (1985), *Beyond the Veil: Male -Female Dynamics in Muslim Society*, rev. ed., London: Al Saqi Books.

Mernissi, F. (1991), *Women and Islam: An Historical and Theological Enquiry*, Oxford: Basil Blackwell.

Muslim (1971), *Sahīh Muslim*, Beirut: Dar al Arabia.

Osiek, C. (1985), 'The Feminist and the Bible: Hermeneutical Alternatives', in A.Y. Collins (ed.), *Feminist Perspectives on Biblical Scholarship*, Chico, CA: Scholar Press.

al-Qardāwi, Yūsuf (1990), *Kaifa nata'āmal ma' as-sunna an-nabawiyya,* Herndon: International Institute for Islamic Thought.

Rippin, A. (1993), *Muslims: Their Religious Beliefs and Practices*, vol. I, London: Routledge.

Roald, A.S. (1994), *Tarbiya: Education and Politics in Islamic Movements in Jordan and Malaysia*, Lund: Almqvist & Wiksell International Lund Studies in History of Religions.

Rosaldo, R. (1993), *Culture and Truth: The Remaking of Social Analysis*, London: Routledge.

Schüssler Fiorenza, E. (ed.) (1994), *Searching the Scriptures,* London: SCM.

Wadud-Muhsin, A. (1992), *Qur'an and Woman*, Kuala Lumpur: Penerbit Fajar Bakti SDN. BHD.

Chapter 2

New Veils and New Voices: Islamist Women's Groups in Egypt

Soroya Duval

'I was educated in a French school, didn't know proper Arabic, and tried a Western life-style. This was the time of my big *Jahiliya*.[1] Fear of God and his mercy took me back to Islam. In Islam I found security, happiness, and truth; the happiness I didn't even feel in the streets of the admired Champs Elysée in Paris' (leader of an Islamist Salafi group).[2]

One might think that in this era of the 'information revolution', Arab Muslim women would be presented in the light of objective and accessible knowledge. However, they tend to be one of the least understood social groups, subjected to speculation, generalization and stereotyping. Analysts inside as well as outside the region tend to regard Muslim women as the most severely oppressed group in present-day society.

The predominance of Islam as well as a common language unifying the huge Arab region are the main reasons for perceiving Arab and Muslim women as a single entity. It is almost impossible to convey a full understanding of gender constructs in the Middle East without coming into collision with the general assumptions and stereotypes held about Islam and Muslim women. A considerable body of new research emerged in the 1980s about women's history in this region, yet with a few exceptions (Hussain 1984; Mohsen 1985; Tucker 1985; Badran 1987; Keddie & Baron 1991; Rosander 1991; Ahmed 1992), the bulk of the studies rest on social development theories, modernization theories, as well as Orientalist or 'neo orientalist' accounts for analyzing Muslim women in the Middle East (Minces 1982;

Nawal el-Sadawi 1980; Atiya 1984; Afshar 1984; Sullivan 1986
1980; Shabaan 1988).

These studies neglect the specificity of Arab history, social
organization and culture. Written from the perspective of
modernization theories such studies emphasize some aspects of
the lives of Arab women at the expense of others. Arab women
are either doomed to an unchanging oppression, or recent changes
are attributed to the transfer of Western ideas. Thus, oppression
is seen as beginning to lift in the nineteenth century with the
coming of Western thought. Western ideas about Islam and
Muslim women date as far back as the seventeenth century, and
have their origin in the tales of travellers or crusaders.
Descriptions of these societies and their custom was mostly
distorted and misconstrued (Said 1978; Akbar 1992). The issue of
women and Islam, however, emerged as central in Western
illustrations when Europeans established themselves as colonial
powers in Muslim countries. In other words the understanding of
women in history suffered from a triple bias, a male bias, a class
bias, and a Western bias. The great variations in the cultures and
societies of the Arab Middle East make any single statement
about Muslim women false and misleading. Arab countries differ
in their history of colonialism, industrialization, urbanization,
modernization, and secularization. Variations are also to be found
in ethnic, tribal, religious, and cultural groups. Likewise, the lives
of women in different classes cannot be considered similar.

Females in the upper and middle classes enjoy more options in
life than women of the lower classes. Nevertheless, Islam is
viewed as the main origin of the prevalence of sexual inequality
in the Middle East. It is, however, a well established fact that
sexual inequality existed in all parts of the world long before the
beginnings of Islam and is therefore not a feature exclusive to
Muslim societies. Analysis of patriarchal notions and institutions
must shift to the fabric of socio-cultural conditions of women's
and men's lives in their different settings. Western social
scientists' approaches reflect a high degree of ethnocentrism in
assuming that liberation for Arab women has to follow the same
unilinear line as the American and European women's movements. It is expected that these goals are universal and that they
should more or less be followed in the same order. However,

some Arab women, mostly of the elite, who have internalized the goals of liberation in another context, do not have the kind of self-image that represents the goal of women's liberation in the West (Ahmed 1992; Joseph 1993). Those women want to retain the communal extended family aspects of traditional society, while eliminating its worst abuses, such as easy divorce for men and forced marriages.

Western feminist researchers in general hold the belief that once a society is dominated in certain spheres by men, women will become a suppressed and passive group. Nothing could be further from the truth according to the Muslim women you will meet in the following passages. Another important arena of social function as well as a sphere of power are women's beliefs and religious activities, which should not be underestimated. Given the general 'Islamic trend' sweeping over the Middle East since the 1970s, they are an interesting realm for analyzing gender struggles in the region. These religious activities involve groups of women between and among whom essential links are created, links which can crosscut and override kin and status group barriers. Female solidarity in the form of 'sub-societies', in social systems where there is a preference for the segregation of the sexes, can be a powerful social force and can become an effective way of enhancing position vis-à-vis the male members of the community.

Female solidarity can also lessen male domination by lowering the degree of dependence that women have on men. I am not suggesting that women's positions should be ranked above that of men's, but that both male and female spheres should be considered carefully, and that such an approach might bring us a long way beyond the stereotype of the meek and subordinate Muslim female. To demonstrate this more effectively, I have taken Egypt as a case study, not only because it is an Arab and predominantly Muslim country, but also because it has played a major role in the struggles around the meanings of gender since the nineteenth century. In many ways developments in Egypt heralded and mirrored developments in the Arab world (Ajami 1981). Secondly, there seems to be a striking similarity between the discourse of the British colonial powers in Egypt during the nineteenth century, and the prevalent feminists today, in which the veil epitomizes Islamic inferiority and the oppression of women

(Ahmed 1992). The colonial power (the British occupation started in 1882) wanted to transform Egyptian society to the values of the 'civilized' European world, and Islam, women, and veiling played a central role in it. In Western eyes only by giving up these 'peculiar' and 'intrinsic' practices, would Muslim societies move forward on the path of civilization. The veil, for the colonizers but also in the vision of contemporary Western political culture, is the most visible marker of the 'otherness' and 'inferiority' of Islamic societies. It therefore was and is an open target for attack and the spearhead of the assault on Muslim societies.

Egypt is particularly interesting because of the various Islamist movements that mushroomed in the 1970s, which also paralleled the formation of Islamist women's groups as part of the broader social movement. I make use of Herbert Blumer's typology of social movements which considers a situation whereby a general social movement can give birth to specific social movements (cited in Turner and Killian 1957: 144-5). It is possible to consider Islamist women groups as one such 'specific social movement', which is advocating an 'Islamic alternative' from a female perspective.

The arguments and empirical data in this article are based on an exploration of the experience of Islamist women in four different groups (Salafi, Tabligh, Zahra, Muslim Brothers), and the part they play in perpetuating or altering relations of power. Participant observation through presence in the meetings or study circles took place, and informal interviews were conducted with leaders as well as members of the groups. I examine what seems to be an ambiguous political struggle by Islamist women, who are on the one hand fighting actively against their inequality but are on the other accepting or supporting their own subordination. Although the location of women's struggles is looked at in a specific cultural setting and is emphasized within the specific interactions of gender, class, and global inequities, I think that the results can be suggestive for understanding women's contradictory role in relations of power elsewhere as well. Further, in an attempt to analyze the Egyptian situation as it developed during the 1970s, the Islamic phenomenon is considered as a processual, multi-dimensional one within the historical framework of factors that encouraged the rise of Islamist women's groups.

The Islamic Trend 'El Tayyar El Islami'

Islamist groups grew stronger and more widespread in the 1970s and have continued to gain ground since. This tendency has made itself visible through the Islamic dress '*El ziyy el Islami*'[3] for both men and women. A variety of factors have contributed to the mushrooming of these groups and the new type of Islamic outlook. Much of the literature dealing with the subject has dated their emergence to the aftermath of the 1967 defeat of Egypt by Israel when people sought a variety of explanations for the humiliating defeat suffered. Common explanations were that the military had grown elitist, corrupt and bureaucratic, or that Egypt was underdeveloped technologically. There was one explanation, however, circulating in the society that was most significant: the Egyptians had abandoned God and, therefore, God had abandoned them.

A further dimension explaining the phenomenon in question was the exploitation or use of religion from above by the government, for purposes of legitimization, as was widely suggested. With regard to the state of unrest prevailing throughout the late 1960s and early 1970s both explanations are valid. Yet in my opinion, the determining factors that permeated Egyptian society favouring an 'Islamic alternative as the way out', and even explicitly used by the Islamists as a slogan 'Islam is the solution' (*Al Islam Huwa El Hall*) are to be found in the period following the 1973 war and all through the decade in question. The Islamic trend was further strengthened spiritually by Iran, Pakistan and Afghanistan. Although these are countries outside the Middle East, they have had tremendous influence, whether formally through groups or informally through the personal attitudes of central political personalities. The Islamic Revolution in Iran 1979, and the Islamization of Pakistan under General Zia ul-Haq after seizing power in 1977, as well as the Afghan mujahedin's struggle against communism, were considered ideals to be followed. The Islamization of Sudan under el-Bashir after seizing power in July 1991 as well as the war in Bosnia are more recent examples.

It is important to note that in our understanding of Islam two equally important levels of analysis present themselves. As Ali Dessouki points out (1982: 14), Islamic experiences are not

historically monolithic. Universality in Islamic history is reflected
and characterized by a prevalent unity of belief whereby the holy
message is operative at the macro level. At the micro level,
however, Islam is specific. Islamic experiences appear therefore
in the shape of activities conditioned by specific cultural and
social constraints.

The Egyptian case is no exception, in that both characteristics
of Islam universalism and specificity — are reflected throughout its
history. The 'Islamic alternative' should not, therefore, be seen as
a novel phenomenon per se although its articulator and the forms
of articulation have changed. The articulation of an 'Islamic
alternative' seems to have been favoured by factors of national
economic and social unrest over the centuries, yet the mani-
festations of these forces have differed from one period to the
next, as have the responses. The challenges faced by Muhammed
Abduh, Rashid Reda, and their disciples at the turn of the century
were different from those that brought about the Hassan al-Banna
movement in the late 1920s and 1930s. Likewise, the mani-
festations of the political, social and economic crisis faced by
Egypt in the 1970s were also different and, consequently, so was
the articulation of the 'Islamic Alternative'.

Nationalism

The loss of faith in Nasser and his entire secularist ideology came
as another consequence of the defeat. His 'socialist' programmes
were now judged to have been failures. After Nasser's death in
1969 the government retreated from socialist politics throughout
the 1970s under Sadat's rule, and Sadat permitted the Muslim
Brothers *(al Ikhwan al Muslimun)* to resume their activities, which
Nasser had banned. Sadat was now increasingly brought under
attack from Nasserists and communists. One strong base of
opposition to his adversaries were the 'Ikhwan' whom Sadat
wanted to exploit to the utmost. Publications by the Muslim
Brothers soon reached a wide audience and, particularly after the
Camp David treaty with Israel, they turned not only to criticizing
Nasserism and communism, but also Sadat's policies. Dissent and
discontent were expressed and formulated in religious language
and terminology. Once they had gained popularity, and afraid of
being called anti-Islamic, Sadat could not afford to strike out

against them. In trying to legitimate his position he also made use of the idiom of religion, declaring himself to be a just Muslim ruler of a state based on the twin pillars of faith (*Iman*) and science (*Ilm*). Conditions meanwhile were such as to breed discontent. The government had embarked on the open-door policy by promulgating new laws to encourage foreign investment, which had adverse effects on the local industries. The country was flooded with luxury and consumer goods far beyond the reach of most Egyptians. The open-door policy brought sudden wealth for a few, together with blatant corruption and avid consumerism. Most Egyptians experienced its negative effects through the government's retreat from internal development and the public sector. Matriculations at the universities continued at a high rate while the public sector, the chief source of employment, was cut back. Unemployment, an unproductive workforce, and the growth of bureaucracy strained government resources.

To ease the strain, laws restricting emigration were relaxed, benefiting the professional classes as well as unskilled workers, who left for the Arab oil states, generally for a limited period of years. Whereas remittances from abroad soon became Egypt's main source of hard currency, unemployment was not reduced, and resulted in a brain drain of the most skilled and employable. Further, returning migrants from the rich oil states, apart from joining the ranks of conspicuous consumerism, returned with an envious resentment of the treatment they had received and the disparity in resources they had observed (Duval 1989). The Camp David accord, which tied Egypt to the United States in favour of alignment with the West and accommodation with Israel, was another major factor fostering discontent. The United States was pouring large aid funds into the country, which created an uneasy political and economic alliance. This alienated Egypt from its traditional place as a leader in the Arab world. This loss increased the opposition of the Islamist groups, who critizized the regime's lack of leadership and moral decay and presented alternatives. In this tense political atmosphere, women's status and family roles were also thrust into the political arena (Ayubi 1980).

The political situation was aggravated even further by economic difficulties, which deprived Egypt of the chance to regain its position of leadership even as it tried to renew its ties to the Arab world. Apart from having a very high foreign debt, Egypt's economy suffers from dependence on remittances and tourism, both of which have fallen in recent years. A major drop in remittances occurred after the Gulf War in 1991 when most migrants returned from Iraq, a major receiver of Egyptian labour. Tourism was greatly affected in 1993, due to the bombing of tourist targets by militant groups which caused a number of tourist fatalities.

In all the Muslim world, the decade of the 1970s seems to have been a period in which religion played the leading role as a means of expressing discontent. Islam has replaced Arab nationalism as the ideology of dissent in the Arab world. In face of present day challenges, nationalism is perceived as inadequate or as having exhausted its purpose. Whatever may be the case, the fact remains that Islam has an undeniable influence on the political process, and has proven to have a strong potential for politicization. This was exemplified in the Iranian Revolution of 1978, the incidents of the grand mosque in Mecca in 1979, and the assassination of President Sadat on 6 October 1981. On the national level, we can follow recent events on the Egyptian political scene. The assassination of Farag Fouda[4] by an Islamic group, the attempted assassination of the Minister of Information on 21 April 1993 and the series of clashes between police and the Islamists in Assiut, Upper Egypt, but also in different quarters in Cairo (Imbaba, Heliopolis), and the series of attacks on tourist targets, amply serve as examples. The confrontation between the police apparatus and the Islamists has reached its peak on the Egyptian political arena. Violence by the regime in the form of mass arrests, mass shootings, imprisonment without trial, torture, death penalties and so on, has created a climate of counter-violence by the militant Islamic groups.[5] The government, in a desperate attempt to stifle even the non-militant Islamic trend that has largely permeated Egypt's syndicates of engineering, medicine, journalism, law, academies and science, has issued a number of decrees to restrict their autonomy and thereby created a general air of discontent among all Islamists.

The Islamic Alternative

During the 1970s, Egypt witnessed more than one group advocating an 'Islamic alternative'. One group of intellectuals exposed and opposed 'Western civilizational imperialism' and called for an Islamic left, *al Yassar al-Islami*. Other groups were the Muslim Brothers, *al Ikhwan al-Muslimun*, the Military Academy (MA), *al Faniyya-al-Askariyya*, the Repentance and Holy Flight group (RHF), *al-Takfir -wal-Hijra*, and the *Jihad* group.[6]

Whereas they differed in their perception of the actual situation that needed to be changed, they basically agreed on the necessity for and the direction of change. Other groups such as Muhammad's Youth, *Shabab Muhammad* and Soldiers of God, *Junud Allah*, also existed. Recently, two groups by the name of *el Shawqiyyin* (in reference to their leader whose name was Shawqi) appeared in Upper Egypt and another one named the Party of God, *Hizballah*, in Alexandria.

By virtue of having engaged at one time or the other in confrontations with the regime as well as through their writings, these groups have attracted public attention. It also has to be kept in mind that there may be groups that have gone underground and of which nothing is known.

I propose to distinguish between groups that I term action-oriented, like those mentioned above, and semi-action oriented groups, like the Salafis, Tabligh, and Zahra. This distinction is important to differentiate them from the less worldly Sufi brotherhoods in Egypt that are non-action oriented, but remain popular. The Salafis,[7] the Tabligh,[8] and the Zahra[9] are groups that have gained tremendous popularity in Egypt. They are interesting not only because of their ideological synthesis between the action-oriented groups and the Sufis, but also because of the emergence of the numerous women's groups within them. The further focus in this article will be on the women in these three groups, as well as the action-oriented Muslim Brothers (*Ikhwan al-Muslimun*).

The Muslim Brothers — Past and Present

The Muslim Brothers were founded by Hassan al-Banna in 1928. They were fiercely anti-British and anti-Western. The movement sought to lead the people back to a purified Islam, which would penetrate every aspect of personal and national life, and free the nation from Western domination. The Muslim Brothers were opposed to the government and the political parties, which they saw as importations of Western ideologies and as tools of British domination. The parties were monopolized by the upper classes, who were participants in and beneficiaries of foreign economic domination. Anger at Western domination and determination to attain independence from it were central to the movement. Al-Banna emphasized the important role of women in the Islamic reformation, and a branch organization, the Society of Muslim Sisters, *El Akhawat El Muslimat* was established. Another Islamist women's organization at that time worth mentioning, is the Muslim Women's Association, which was founded by the Islamist Zeinab al-Ghazali in 1936. Al-Ghazali, although independent, supported the cause of the Muslim Brothers, and the definition of the role of women in an Islamic society coincides with that expressed by the Muslim Brothers: 'Islam does not forbid women to actively participate in public life. It does not prevent her from working, entering into politics, and expressing her opinion, or from being anything as long as that does not interfere with her first duty as a mother, the one who first trains her children in the lslamic call.' Al-Ghazali's increased cooperation with the Muslim Brothers was interrupted by the intense persecution of the Brothers, as well as by the murder of Hassan al-Banna in 1949. She herself was imprisoned and tortured for six years (1965-72) at the hands of the Nasser regime. The Muslim Women's Association continued to function until her imprisonment in 1965, when it was dissolved. It has not been reconstituted since, though al-Ghazali continues to lecture and work for the Islamic cause. A few months ago, a newspaper by the name of *Al-Usra-Al-Arabia* (The Arabic Family) opened in which Ghazali was active. It was issued by the Muslim Brothers, but was quickly banned by the government after four issues.

The Muslim Brothers epitomize the most important development in the 1980s. They have progressed beyond preaching towards institutionalization, and are committed to the establishment of an Islamic socio-political order based on Islamic law *(Sharia).* This progression has made itself felt in two ways. The first was their sophisticated participation in the parliamentary elections of 1984 and 1987 and thereby their acceptance of political pluralism. Secondly, they gradually but steadily established an Islamic infrastructure which includes schools, hospitals, clinics, investment houses and other commercial enterprises. In contrast to the services provided by the government, these enterprises are cleaner, sometimes cheaper, and less bureaucratized. Thus, compared to what are known as the *Infitah* or open-door enterprises, they increasingly gained in popularity. This rapidly mushrooming infrastructure has undoubtedly given the government some breathing space, but has also increased the popularity of the Muslim Brothers even more.

Joining the *Jihad* group in the 1970s was one alternative to express frustration and dissatisfaction, whereas in the mid 1980s joining the Muslim Brotherhood was a more attractive, less demanding, more comfortable and respectable alternative. Their efficiency in stretching out their hands to the masses in times of crisis reached its peak after the devastating earthquake of October 1992. The ability of the Muslim Brothers to mobilize their network instantly to provide food and shelter for the poor and homeless whose houses had collapsed, exposed the government's inefficiency and its meager and belated efforts. The political triumph achieved by the Muslim Brothers sufficiently alarmed the government — especially as elections were coming up — that it struck out against the Brothers by issuing a number of decrees to limit the autonomy of the unions and syndicates that had become increasingly Islamized. This, in my opinion, increased anew the appeal of the violence-oriented groups, and can be witnessed in the increasing violence used by these groups in Egypt.

Ideology of Semi-action Groups

Whereas the Sufis have a strong belief in saints and their ability to influence or affect personal destinies through their prayers to God (*karamat*), and usually visit their shrines and ask for their help and blessings through their special connection with God, the semi-action-oriented groups reject these beliefs with repugnance:

It is totally forbidden and sinful *(haram)* to worship saints and ask them for things, or even have the remotest belief that they can intervene in our destiny. This is a form of heresy *(shirk)*. Islam is built on the Oneness of God *(Tawhid)*. Only God can make our destiny, only God can alter it, and it is only Him we should ask help or forgiveness. There is no intermediary between any person and God. The people who do this are

ignorant and don't know their religion properly (interview with member
of Tabligh group).

The Sufis believe in a vertical and personal relationship between
the individual and God which is strengthened through worship and
prayer. Ultimate happiness and peace are the fruits of such a
bond, but are also rewarded in the Hereafter. Therefore, for the
Sufi, worldly matters including the conditions of state or society
are of minor importance as long as inner peace is reached. Unlike
other parts of Africa or in the Maghreb where Sufis were politically active, the Sufi groups in Egypt are totally depoliticized and
are in no way a threat to the regime. On the other hand, for the
Salafis, the Zahra, and the Tabligh, societal change is one of the
main aims strived for, but it can only be reached by the inner
transformation of oneself. All Muslims should unite to bring about
a society governed by the ethics of Islam to ensure justice and
equality for all.

'If everyone follows the deeds of the Prophet Muhammad, no
human being would harm the other, and there would be no evil'
(Tabligh member). Although the Salafis and the Tabligh are not
in open confrontation with the regime as they avoid any political
involvement in the form of speeches or writings, yet they criticize
the reluctance of the government to implement the Islamic Law
(*Sharia*) in all aspects of life, the increased corruption and moral
decay that is apparent in Egypt, and the immoral behaviour among
men and women in a mixed environment. 'Just look at the
crowded buses where men and women stick to each other, and
any man putting his filthy hands wherever he pleases on any
woman. Do you call this liberation or development for women'
(Tabligh member)?

These groups, though totally incapable of destabilizing the
regime in any way, were encouraged by the government in order
to play down the growing voice of the *Ikhwan al-Muslimun* who
were more action-oriented and in open opposition to the government.

However, recent arrests of members of these groups and
allegations of social disorder might be a sign of their increased
politicization. Meanwhile, media coverage and TV programmes
on prime time were suddenly opened to a number of *Salafi*
leaders who propagated their ideas via TV, video tapes, books,

magazines, tapes, and religious study groups in homes and mosques.

These groups share with the Sufis the notion of self-discipline and purification of oneself from previous sins. The focus of change lies in the inner being, which would then reflect on the outside, and eventually on the whole society. One of the members summed this idea up by quoting a verse from the Koran: 'God would not change a community unless they change what is in themselves' (*Lajughajer Allah ma bi qawmen hata jughayyiru ma bi anfusihim*). Change is considered an inner process growing gradually to the outside: 'Everyone should start by himself, and ask himself how the Prophet Muhammad was, and how his followers (*Sahaba*) were, and try to be like them. Only then, when they follow the teachings of the Prophet can they tell other people what to do and order them to do the good and leave the evil' (*amr bil marouf wa al nahiy an el mounkar*) (Member of Salafi).

Muslim Sisters

Women's groups affiliated to the Muslim Brothers were more engaged in direct politics than women of the other semi-action oriented groups. A number of them were members of the People's Party *El-Shaab* (previously socialist, but now increasingly Islamist). Most of these women have a higher degree of education and are in some form or another related to the academia, which makes the form of teaching and discussions more intellectual and sophisticated, rather than the oversimplified logic presented in the other groups.

Local newspapers are regularly and carefully read by these women. The mastering of at least one foreign language (French, English, German) gives them access to the international debates and discourses in the different media. They are thus able to form a more holistic picture of how Egypt fits into the global world system.

> During the whole of last week, there was nothing in the government newspapers except how Mubarak was cordially received in the USA on his trip, and how the United States desperately looked forward to his visit. In reality Mubarak's visit received very little coverage in the Western mass media in general, and what they did say about Mubarak and his

policies was not that positive although he is perceived as the 'hero' or 'champion' of what they call 'moderate' Islam and 'democratic' Egypt. In fact, Clinton didn't spend more than fifteen minutes with Mubarak. That's how cordially he was received (comment from member of *Ikhwan*).

Women in the *Ikhwan* group, see it as the duty of devoted Muslims to change the society around them into a more just and egalitarian form that matches Islamic perceptions. They express their ideas in meetings, gatherings, public lectures, and writings.

It is our duty as Muslim women to have a say in the politics of our country and the politics that shape our lives as women. Politics is not only the realm of men, as many men want to propagate. On the contrary, it has been made our primary concern throughout Islamic history since 1500 years ago, when the women gave the Prophet their vote (*Baiya*) personally. We were equally addressed, and were equal partners in matters of the state. This is, however, not the notion most Muslim men carry. Somewhere, the perception of women being only bodies fit for the kitchen or the bed lingers in the back of their heads (leader in *Ikhwan*).

Social Profile

These women's groups gathered mainly for educational purposes like reading, explaining the Koran and the Sayings (Hadith) of the Prophet. At the beginning of my attendances at group meetings, the personal atmosphere towards me was one of suspicion and reluctance. My affiliation to a foreign institution in Sweden and my partly European origin seemed to be drawbacks. The potential use of this research was put into question, and questions were posed as to whether the idea of doing it was mine, assigned to me, or proposed by members of my department or university. Taking the constraining political situation into account, this attitude was hardly surprising. Perhaps also the somewhat justifiable conspiratorial theory deeply rooted in Muslims through the history of the crusades, latter's hostility towards anything even remotely related to Islam, and the continuation of this hostility in a different form in the contemporary political culture of the West, has contributed to a powerful rejection of Western culture or ideals.

We don't want the West, and we don't care about the West or what they think of us. They have a hatred in their hearts against us that is blinding them and blocking their hearts and minds from any understanding of how we want to live. So is the case of all unbelievers who have sickness in their hearts. By the will of God, we will have victory over them (member of Tabligh).

In any case, trying to penetrate a world that was courteous yet continuously on guard was a difficulty I had to cope with at the start. Being a Muslim myself helped in becoming more familiar with the women, suspicions slowly eroded, and a trusting relationship was established. In this context my foreign affiliation and origin proved to be helpful. In fact, they were able to draw on any identity they liked, depending on the situation.

The meetings were generally held twice a week and took place in mosques as well as in homes. Usually the leader and two or three other women would be responsible for the lecture. Sometimes, Islamist women from outside the group, like former actresses, would be invited to talk. There has been a vogue for Egyptian actresses to Islamicize; some of them abandoning their acting career whilst at the height of success. These women are looked at with a sense of euphoria and are taken as symbols of how fame, beauty, wealth and power are not comparable to the beauty, wealth, and power of Islam. As a member of Salafi stated; 'Shams (a former actress) had fame, beauty and everything she could ever wish for, but she discarded everything and chose Islam. In it she found real happiness. This is the real example we should follow.'

Although the meetings included women from all strata of the society, there was a heavy middle-class presence. All age groups were represented, with a predominance in age group between twenty to thirty. Single as well as married women flocked to the meetings. Another interesting characteristic was the appearance of many different forms of veils, as well as women who were bare headed. Women in the *Tabligh* and *Salafi* groups usually tend to wear a face-cover (*Niqab*), whereas the *Zahra* women usually have a form of headscarf, and the *Ikhwan* prefer a large headscarf covering the breasts or reaching even to the waist called *Khimar*. This distinction, however, could not be made among the groups as all variations existed and there was no clear-cut line. The majority of the women attending were not aware or did not think it important to know to which Islamic tendency the group belonged.

Regular attendance in a group was based on adherence to the general Islamic trend (*El-Tayyar-El-Islami*). The psychological and social dimensions are given as among the most important elements promoting adherence. Inner calm and resolution, often described as a feeling of inner peace brought about by formal or public alignment with Islam, are prominent in the women's accounts (Radwan 1992). This conclusion conforms to the findings of this study. Women often stated that 'they had become calmer with their husbands', 'were able to deal better with family problems' and 'weren't easily bothered by minor things like before'. They also felt a sense of community and of communality of values that comforted them. There was a big emphasis on sisterhood and love for one another in the name of God (*El Hub Fil Lah*). This was to be the main form of group interest or solidarity regardless of any material or personal interest. A member of Tabligh expressed it in this way: '*El Hub Fil Lah* is the purest and most sincere form of love, because I don't love you for being rich or beautiful, but because you share with me the love of God.'

Their talk revolved mostly around Islam, apart from inquiring about each other's health and children. They were urged to read more and to be active and they did not indulge in light conversation, which according to them is a waste of time. A common theme in the lectures was presented as follows: 'We as Muslim women should get prepared and equip ourselves with knowledge to preach Islam. Muslim women should not sit for hours in front of the TV. Our main concern should be *Dawa*: to preach Islam and invite other people to Islam, not to watch "The Bold and the Beautiful"' (leader of *Zahra*).

Another common theme is the emphasis on Islam as a religion as well as a state *(Din wa Dawla)* regulating all aspects of life and opposed to the secular 'immoral' West where there is a separation between state and church. The Western lifestyle is often put into stark contrast with Islam. TV serials like Dallas and 'The Bold and the Beautiful' shown on Egyptian TV give further inspiration:

Now the West worships a new kind of God. Their God is called 'do anything you like'. There are no rules or limits. Men and women go around almost naked in the streets, they kiss and touch each other in public, and in the name of liberty they sleep around as they like. Women are exposing that which should be private as a cheap commodity to anyone. Can this be called women's liberation, civilization or development? The West is disintegrating, and their people are lost amidst high crime rates, drugs and sexual perversity. Islam prevents all this (member of Ikhwan).

The *Nef*-Veil

Veiling is now common among university students and young professionals. The Islamic trend has become more prevalent among men and women in both categories. Whereas the term *muhajjabat* in Arabic means the 'veiled ones', the veil does not necessarily have to cover the face. However, both sexes should meet the Islamic requirements of modesty in dress, in the sense that it should not be sexually enticing. Robes should be loose fitting, long-sleeved and ankle length, and should not reveal the contours of the body. Conforming to this code, men and women have developed styles of dress that are actually quite new. It is neither the traditional dress of Egypt, nor Western, nor Arabian, although all three elements might combine. For women, depending on how modesty is defined, a variety of headgear and face coverings with different colours and thickness of material is observed. Men may wear baggy trousers and loose shirts.

Islamic dress is also a way of affirming ethical and social customs. Mixing among the sexes in universities and in workplaces, as is the social reality in Egypt today, becomes less offensive. As one observer of the Islamic phenomenon put it, in adopting Islamic dress women 'are carving out legitimate public space for themselves', and public space is by this means being redefined to accommodate women (Al-Guindi 1981). The adoption of the dress does not declare women's place to be at home, but on the contrary legitimizes their presence outside it. Consequently, the prevalence of the Islamic mode among women cannot be seen as a retreat from female autonomy and subjectivity. The availability of education, the entry of women into universities and professional occupations cannot be considered regressive, no matter how conservative the appearance of the uniform that helps them to achieve these goals may look. Islamist women are also invading the mosques, previously a male domain. Some men may resist the sharing of their power, but at the same time they are defenceless as the process is taking place within the legitimate dominant culture. The charge of being anti-Islamic by not supporting the women in the Islamic trend is an accusation most men don't want to be confronted with. Women are not only making use of this political space, but are constantly equipping themselves with examples from Muslim women in Islamic history which are used to legitimize their position:

Aisha, the wife of the Prophet transmitted three quarters of the *Hadith* (sayings of the Prophet), she was on the battlefield side by side with the Prophet, and even led a war against Ali after the Prophet's death. When Umar Ibn El Khattab wanted to deprive Aisha from performing the pilgrimage, she resisted fiercely. We as Muslim women should follow her path (leader of Zahra).

Another member of the Ikhwan said: 'During the time of the Prophet women attended the prayers from dawn to sunset. No man has the right to deprive a woman from her Islamic mission. Submissiveness is only to God and not to any human being (*La Taata Li Makhlouk Fi Maseyyet El Khaleq*). A Muslim woman should fight for her rights, even if this means in some cases divorce.'

Using this pretext, women's freedom of mobility has increased. They are able to move freely, attend lessons and weddings with the other sisters, without requiring the consent of their husbands, fathers, or brothers. Similarly a member of a Salafi group expressed her anger at a man who didn't want her to attend to her lesson with a group of children in the main part of the mosque — usually the men's domain.

It was degrading and humiliating the way this man looked at me, as if I were nothing — a piece of garbage. He waved at me with his hands as if he was scaring off a little dog and ordered me to confine myself to the women's quarters which is very small and terribly hot now in summer. I thought to myself, I am wearing the Islamic dress, and am totally respectable in every way, so I just gave him my back and ignored him totally. I heard him mumbling in anger and then he went away. I think he learned a lesson he will never be able to forget.

The leader of the Salafi group mentioned a sit-in in the men's part of the mosque, when a man shouted at them from behind the curtain to lower their voices. 'We should demonstrate for our rights and next time make the lesson in the men's quarters in order to have more space. They are not going to die if they switch to our place twice a week.'

The Islamic dress also brings a variety of practical advantages for women. On the simplest level, it is economical; women are saved the expense of acquiring fashionable clothes and having more than two or three outfits. The dress also protects them from male harassment. 'Being totally covered saves me from the approaches of men and hungry looks. I feel more free, purer, and more respectable' (member of Tabligh).

That *El-Ziyy El-lslami* does not resemble traditional dress is perhaps a significant fact. In modern times traditional dress has come to be confined to the lower classes and the peasantry, and therefore identifies the wearer as being from these classes, whereas *El-Ziyy-El-Islami* might be seen as a democratic dress that to a large extent erases class origins. In previous fieldwork conducted in rural Egypt, a peasant woman pronounced these class distinctions clearly: 'Only educated women can wear the *Hijab*, but if a peasant woman wears it, people will make fun of her.' The wearing of Islamic dress and Islamism as a dominant discourse of social being is marked by a vocabulary of dress and social being defined from below by the emerging middleclasses rather than by the formerly culturally dominant upper classes.

Renegotiation of Gender Relations

The *Hijab* voices the protest that many women dare not voice directly to their husbands, and perhaps that many can not articulate completely even to themselves. 'The lecturing, reading, and the many activities with the sisters make me very busy, and most of the time the house is in a mess, but my husband doesn't get angry because he knows my Islamic obligations' (leader in Ikhwan). 'Men should help women in housework. Any man is not better than the Prophet who used to bake the bread and sew his own garment when cut' (member of Salafi).

Although women's protest might be indirect and displaced into the symbolic realm, the previous statements by women can be read as signs that significant negotiations of power are taking place. Through veiling women's protests can be voiced and perhaps ameliorated in at least three dimensions of inequality: in relations of gender, class, and global position. In the realm of gender, for instance, these women are perceiving a different womanhood, they are hearing the ethical, just, egalitarian voice of Islam and are demanding its implementation in their family politics. By singling out elements from Islamic history, or as one woman said 'educate women in what their real rights are in Islam', Islamist women are indeed starting to challenge the androcentric dominant culture of established Islam that is hostile to women, and the language of the politically dominant. Central issues, such as marriage and divorce and the custody of children, are looked at from Islamicized women's perspective. Islamist women claim, for example, that any conditions can be stipulated by the woman who wishes to protect her rights in the marriage. This may include the freedom of choice in working or not, restriction of polygamy, and custody over future children. The fear of men's easy divorce from women (as occurs now in established Islam), or of no possibility of divorce when the wife asks for it, as dissolution of the marriage contract lies in the hands of men, is considered a distortion of Islam brought about by some male Islamic scholars *(ulama)* as well as by men who did not understand Islam properly and abused these rights. A practical solution within accessible political reach is to give the wife full autonomy to dissolve the marriage contract herself without waiting for the husband's consent. This was spelled out in the teachings of Muhammad Abduh, an Islamic scholar in the nineteenth century, as well as by one of the first Islamist feminists, Zeinabal-Ghazali, but also in the early Islam of the seventh century, and was therefore considered totally legitimate.

In the area of class relations, the veil is a very potent signal. The veil allies modest middle-class women and differentiates them from lower-class women. There is also a strongly felt anger over the loss of traditional values that has accompanied the overwhelming thrust of modernization and development, and which is epitomized in veiling and Islamism. In reaffirming the values they hold as important and in an attempt to make them real again, identifying themselves with Islam shows their connection to a vibrant and powerful culture, a culture they wish to hold on to, as opposed to the invading culture of the West. For Islamist women this nationalistic and anti-Western aspect has been perhaps the most salient. What they are actually protesting against is the vision of womanhood presented by the West, the image of the future imposed by modernization, and the inflation caused by economic dependency on other powers.

'Modernizing' Women

Middle Eastern societies began undergoing a fundamental social transformation at the end of the eighteenth and beginning of the nineteenth century. Foreign colonial powers dominated the area whether formally or informally, and by the economic encroachment of the West, the region was incorporated into the world economic system. 'Modern' states emerged, and were the paramount political transformation. This period witnessed enormous vitality in the literary, intellectual, social, and political life of women. For the first time women emerged as a significant subject for national debate. Issues of polygamy, the treatment of women in Muslim custom, easy male access to divorce and segregation were ventilated openly for the first time. These issues were initially raised by Egyptian male intellectuals, and were intertwined with nationalism as well as social and cultural reforms that they believed were important for national 'advancement'

Qasim Amin, an Egyptian French-educated upper-class lawyer, was one of the first towards the end of the nineteenth century to write a book where he called for the unveiling and liberation of Egyptian women. Amin's book, 'Women's Liberation' (*Tahrir El Mar'a*, 1899) marks the entry of the debate around the veil, in which the veil epitomized Islamic inferiority. This debate was incorporated into mainstream Arabic discourse that has recurred in a variety of forms in a number of Muslim and Arab countries since then. Amin's call for unveiling was followed by many in Egypt, typically from an upper-class background and with some degree or other Western affiliation.

The discussion of women and reform was mostly linked to the 'advancement' of European society and the need for Muslims to catch up. The new discourse that emerged connected nationalism with women and cultural change rather than displacing the classical formulations on gender. Nevertheless, the first three decades of the century marked a feminism that was visible intellectually, organizationally, and politically. Women started to contribute intellectually by founding and writing in a variety of women's journals, and organizations for the intellectual improvement of women appeared. Politically, they were members of women's political organizations paralleling and actively supporting men's parties. The first feminist discourses and feminist analysis observed in this period, all originated from women from upper-class backgrounds.

Although these women marked a change in women's opportunities, yet like Amin they were mostly Westward-looking, affiliated themselves to the West, and adopted an outlook that valorized Western ways as more advanced and more 'civilized' than native ways. Well-known names of feminists of this period are Malak Hifni Nassef, Huda Sha'rawi, Saiza Nabarawi, Doria Shafik, and Mai Ziyada who pushed for fundamental reforms in the laws governing women. They demanded education and suffrage rights for all women. This was achieved after Egypt expelled the British and proclaimed itself a Republic with a new constitution in 1956. The monarchy was terminated by a military coup launched by the Free Officers in 1952. King Farouk was exiled and Nasser was brought to power.

Huda Sha'rawi, the pre-eminent feminist leader of the twenties and thirties, founded the Egyptian Feminist Union (EFU) in 1923, the first Pan-Arab feminist movement in Egypt. The 1920s movement by Egyptian feminists like Huda Sha'rawi and Saiza Nabarawi to discard the veil remained primarily an upper-class phenomenon. It was linked with upper-class women's entrance into political life through participation in the struggles of Egyptian nationalist groups and political efforts to rid the country of the foreign presence. Sha'rawi was a member of the upper classes, and from a very early age, she had been guided in her thoughts and readings by Eugenie Le Brun, a French woman. Le Brun had conveyed to Sha'rawi the common European belief that 'the veil stood in the way of their (Egyptian women's) advancement' (Badran 1987). Thus in the early twentieth century, and mainly through the EFU, the Westernizing voice of feminism emerged as the uncontested and dominant voice of feminism in the Arab context. It affiliated itself with the Westernizing, secularizing tendencies in society, predominantly the tendencies of the upper and upper-middle classes, and promoted a feminism that assumed the desirability of progress toward Western-type societies.

However, as mentioned earlier, another totally different tone of feminism existed at the time. It was the strain of feminism promoted by Zeinab al-Ghazali who founded the Islamic Women's Association. Al-Ghazali campaigned for women and the nation in Islamist terms, whereas the other feminists at the time campaigned for women's rights and human rights in the language of secularism and democracy. Whereas these feminists consistently stressed the superiority of the West in their feminist goals and actions, Al-Ghazali was committed to indigenous culture and to pursuing feminism in indigenous terms. She was determined to find feminism within Islam, and this is juxtaposed to the adulation of the West and the undermining of the native that formed the discourse of the other feminists. In advocating reformist ideas similar to Muhammed Abduh's reformist ideas of Islam in the nineteenth century, she articulated a belief in a reformist Islam which also favoured women.

Until the last decades of the century, the dominant voice of feminism in Egypt as well as in the Middle East was of a Western type, whereas this second strand remained marginal. It was seen only as an alternative and was not even recognized as a voice of feminism. Ironically, as this century draws to its end, it is the feminism advocated by Zeinab al-Ghazali which seems to capture the hearts and minds of the Islamist women. It apparently has greater resonance for the shaping of mainstream Egyptian culture, whereas the indisputably dominant voice of secularist, Westernizing Arab feminism has become the marginal and alternative voice. In seeking to decode the reasons for the Islamic trend, numerous sociological endeavours are focused on such dichotomies as nation-state/civil society, tradition/modernity, a kind of 'Glaubenskrieg' between South and North, core/periphery, capitalist/pre-capitalist, rural/urban and so on. Whatever the fabrics involved in feeding this process, it is obvious that the language of Western-type feminism has exhausted its purposes.

Conclusion

The idea that improving the status of Arab or Muslim or other non-Western women requires them to abandon their own native customs is still prevalent in most Western feminist discourses. Analysts treat the debate as one between feminists, that is, Amin and his allies, and 'anti-feminists', meaning Amin's critics. Taking these postures, they automatically accept the supposition made by Amin and the Western discourse: that the veil is a symbol of oppression. Consequently, those who called for its abandonment were feminists, whereas those rejecting that call, were anti-feminists. Assumptions are made by such feminists that the adoption of Islamic dress, because it reflects 'conservative' and ethical social habits, also automatically denotes support of male dominance and female subservience. The possible 'feminist' positions taken by women adopting Islamic dress, positions supportive of female autonomy and equality, are articulated in terms totally different from the language of Western and Western-affiliated feminism. Investigators of the phenomenon must try to decipher this language in order to make an understanding possible. In times of social change and political opportunity there is an even possibility of inequalities either being reproduced or totally altered.

The logic of reproduction and real change are the same, and each time that a political opening arises, either result is a possibility. Just as the acquiescent aspects of women's behaviour can be singled out for co-option, so could the protesting elements be encouraged and developed. The Islamist women I came to know are involved in important choices in a struggle to define both their own identity and women's place in a changing society. They are attempting to discover an appropriate identity which fits their tradition as it redefines their future, which has also been the longer struggle of the Arab world. Negotiating their future is the task these women confront with their invasion of 'public space', whatever form this may take.

Fox Genovese (1991), writing on US society, observes that 'sexism instead of receding with the triumph of modernity, has probably become more general and more difficult to locate in a single institution'. She also confirms that late capitalist society 'has contributed a bitter twist to the centuries of female oppression'. Similarly, Michel Foucault articulated the view that modern forms of power are much more difficult to locate as they lack a center, or an 'eye' (Foucault 1972). In this context, Michel de Certeau (1984) argues that subordinate groups turn to the use of small tactics as the only viable form of protest to bargain over modern forms of power. In the end, however, they might form a significant resistance, a strategy that is likely to be adopted by these women in their future struggle.

Notes

1. *Jahiliya*, literally ignorance, but in Islamic history referred to as the period of worshipping idols in pre-Islamic Arabia.
2. Interview conducted by author in 1993.
3. The term signifies that they fulfil Islamic requirements of modesty.
4. Faraq Fouda was a secular anti-Islamist writer.
5. A group called *Jihad,* whose spiritual leader Omar Abd Errahman is currently living in exile in the United States, has taken responsibility for some of the killings and bombings. It is the most militant group operating in Egypt today and is usually blamed by the media for any unrest created.
6. *Jihad* means struggle or enormous effort to achieve a religious cause. It is important to note that these groups do not call themselves RHF, MA or Jihad. These are names given to them by the authorities and the media. Members of the Jihad for example call themselves the Islamic group of Egypt, *Al Jamaa al-Islamiyya fi Misr.*
7. Salafis or Salatiyyin means the righteous followers of the 'Salaf el-Saleh' the true believers in the Prophet's time and after. Their loyalty is towards Saudi Arabia and their Ulama (religious scholars), as is the form of Islam they are conveying.
8. Tabligh, literally to inform (in Arabic). It is their duty to tell about Islam.
9. A group originally initiated by a Syrian woman in Syria. In Syria it might have a different name, in Egypt it calls itself Zahra. They have an Islamic women's organization in Cairo that they also call Zahra in reference to the daughter of the prophet Muhammad, Fatima el Zahra.

References

Abbot, N. (1942), *Aishah the Beloved of Muhammed,* Chicago: University Press of Chicago.

Abdallah, A. (1993), 'Islamist and the State', *Middle East report,* vol. 23, no. 183.

Abdel-Hamid, Fathi-Mursi (1981), *Huda Sha'rawi, uthakirat huda Sha'rawi,* Cairo: al-Hilal.

Abdel Kadar, S. (1982), 'The Image of Women in Drama & Women's Programs on Egyptian TV', Ph.D. dissertation, Cairo University.

Adel-Fattah, N. (1984), *Al Moshaf Wal Seif* (The Holy Book and the Sword), Cairo: Madbouli.

Afshar, H. (1984), 'Muslim Women and the Burden of Ideology', in H. Afshar (ed.), *Iran: A Revolution in Turmoil,* London: Macmillan.

Ahmed, L. (1992), *Women and Gender in Islam. Historical roots of a Modern Debate.* New Haven and London: Yale University Press.

Ajami, F. (1981), *The Arab Predicament,* Cambridge: Cambridge University Press.

Akbar, A.S. (1992), *Postmodernism and Islam. Predicament and Promise,* London: Routledge.

Atiya, N. (1982), *Khul-Khaal: Five Egyptian Women Tell Their Stories,* New York: Syracuse University Press.

Ayubi, N.M. (1980), 'The Political Revival of Islam', *International Journal of Middle East Studies,* vol. 12, no. 4.

Badran, M. (1987), *Harem Years: The Memoirs of an Egyptian Feminist,* New York: Feminist Press.

Baron, B. (1988), 'Unveiling in Early Twentieth Century Egypt: Practical and Symbolic Considerations', *Middle Eastern Studies,* vol. 25, no. 3.

De Certeau, M. (1984), 'Des espaces et des pratiques', *La Culture au pluriel,* Paris: Union Général d'éditions.

Dessouki, A. (1982), *Islamic Resurgence in the Arab World,* New York: Praeger Publishers.

Duval, S. (1989), *Socio-economic Effects of Labour Migration on Women and Children in Egypt,* Department of Sociology Lund.

Foucault, M. (1972), *Power/Knowledge,* New York: Pantheon.

Fox-Genovese, E. (1991), *Feminism without Illusions: A Critique of Individualism*, Chapel Hill: University of North Carolina Press.

Al-Ghazali (1976), *Ayyam Min Hayyati,* Cairo: Dar El Shuruq.

Graham-Brown, S. (1994), *Women and Politics in the Middle East,* Special MERIP publication.

Al-Guindi, F. (1981), 'Veiling Infitah with Muslim Ethic', *Social Problems,* vol. 28, no. 4.

Hussain, F. (ed.) (1984), *Muslim Women*, New York: St.Martin's Press.

Joseph, S. (1994), *Gender and Family in the Arab World,* Special MERIP publication.

Keddie N. & B. Baron (1991), *Women in Middle Eastern History: Shifting Boundaries in Sex and Gender,* New Haven and London: Yale University Press.

Krämer, G. (1993), 'Islamist Notions of Democracy', *Middle East Report,* July-August no. 183, vol. 23, no. 4.

Lerner, D. (1958), *The Passing of Traditional Society: Modernizing the Middle East,* New York: Free Press.

Marshall, S. (1984), 'Paradoxes of Change: Culture, Crisis, Islamic Revival and the Reactivation of Patriarchy', *Journal of Asian and African Studies,* no. 19, vols. 1 & 2.

Minces, J. (1982), *The House of Obedience,* London: Zed Press.

Mohsen, S. (1985), 'New Images Old Reflections: Working Middle-Class Women Egypt', in Ferena, E. (ed.) *Women and the Family in the Middle East*, Austin, Tex.: University of Texas Press.

Nawal, Y. (1982), *Kvinnan under Islam,* Stockholm, Røda Rummet: Prinkipo Press.

Radwan, Z. (1992), *Thahirat Al-Hijjab*, Cairo: Behouth al Jenaia.

Rosander, Evers E. (1991), *Women in Borderland: Managing Muslim Identity where Morocco meets Spain,* Stockholm: Gotab.

Saad, E.I. (1981), *The New Social Order.* Boulder, CO: Westview Press; London: Croom Helm.

el-Saadawi, N. (1980), *The Hidden Face of Eve,* Boston: Beacon Press.

Saalman, M. 'The Arab Women', *Women in the Middle East,* London: Zed Books.

Al-Said (1977), *Hassan al-Banna,* Cairo: Madbouli.

Said, E. (1978), *Orientalism,* New York: New York Vintage Books.

Sami, Z. (1980) (1992), MERIP Reports November/December, no. 179, vol. 22.

Shaaban, B. (1988), *Both Right and Left Handed: Arab Women Talk about their Lives,* London: The Women's Press.

Sivan, E. (1985), *Radical Islam,* New Haven: Yale University Press.

Spivak, G. (1987), *In Other Worlds: Essays in Cultural Politics,* New York: Mathew Bell Books.

Sullivan, E. (1986), *Women in Egyptian Public Life,* New York: Syracuse University Press.

Toubia, N. (ed.) (1988), *Women of the Arab World,* New Jersey: Zed Press.

Tucker, J. (1985), *Women in Nineteenth Century Egypt,* Cambridge: Cambridge University Press.

Tucker, J. (1993), *Arab Women: Old Boundaries New Frontiers,* Indiana University Press.

Turner, R.H. & L.M. Killian (1957), *Collective Behaviour,* New Jersey: Prentice Hall.

Webster, S. (1984), 'Harim and Hijab: Elusive and Exclusive Aspects of Traditional Muslim Identity', *Women Studies International Forum,* vol. 7, no. 4.

Wikan, U. (1982), *Behind the Veil in Arabia,* Baltimore: John Hopkins University Press.

Zenie-Ziegler, W. (1988), *In Search of Shadows: Conversations with Egyptian Women,* New Jersey: Zed Books.

Chapter 3

Contested Identities: Women and Religion in Algeria and Jordan

Wilhelmina Jansen

Woman and Muslim. Conflicting or Complementary Identities?

The Islamic resurgence in the Middle East has led many women to shifts in perceptions of self as women and as Muslims. Their established identities are contested by new religious leaders who through the media and social control impose a 'new' identity for Muslims with specific notions of gender and gender relations as important elements. As a result, women question whether their gender identity, how they feel, behave and represent themselves as women, is still in line with the propagated Muslim identity.

Based on data gathered during anthropological fieldwork in Jordan and Algeria, this paper looks at how women try to re-concile new notions of femininity with a new identity as Muslims. On the theoretical level it discusses how people's multiple identities continually contest each other and how this must be taken into account in a theory of identity formation. It is also argued that insight in this process is essential to understanding women's participation in fundamentalist movements.

Introduction

'You are accountable for none but yourself' (Koran 4: 83).

Aisha, a Jordanian woman of 23, is trying out new ways to present herself. It is spring 1989, a few weeks before the start of Ramadan. The coming of the month of fast has touched a deeply hidden religious spot in her. Up till then she considered herself a young carefree woman, outgoing and attractive, a Muslim, but not thinking about Islam too much. She worked as a secretary to the Jordanian television station in Amman when she met her college-educated husband. The marriage was not as traditional as that of some of her sisters and friends: hers was not arranged by senior family members, the couple were not related, they did not move in with the husband's family but established themselves independently, and she did not stay home but found a new job as a secretary at the university in a nearby town. Aisha continued to dress and wear make-up as she was used to doing as a girl and helped her husband make professional videos, including one which propagated birth control. When her second daughter was born she quit her job to take better care of her children. Now, after some months of being a full-time mother and housewife she decides that it is time 'to become serious' as she calls it.

But becoming serious is not without problems. She has many questions to ask friends, relatives and me to determine how to become a good Muslim and to start being accountable for herself. Most questions concern the modesty of her attire: 'Do you think the flowers on this scarf are too colourful?' 'Shouldn't I wear the scarves I have rather than bring my husband to new expenses?' 'Is this dress too bright?' 'Can I wear high heels with a jellaba?' She also starts to question her previous behaviour: 'Can I still take the bus to town with my mother-in-law?' or 'Maybe I was wrong to have put in an I.U.D. before giving my husband a son.' In the course of redefining her own proper behaviour, she also reconsidered the proper upbringing of her daughters: 'Is it bad to let my daughter ride a bike?' (As a non-Muslim I could not always give proper Islamic advice, only to the last question I convincingly argued that there was nothing wrong with a three-year-old pedalling her three-wheeled bike on the porch).[1]

Many women like Aisha follow and support the religious revival in Muslim countries, and in doing so ask advice from relatives, peers and new religious leaders, and thus contribute to the proliferation of religious books, pamphlets, cassettes, television and radio programmes and study groups where questions of religion and morality are discussed. A growing number of women turn away from their previous way of living and behaving and more or less adhere to 'fundamentalist' ideas.[2] At first sight there seems to be a complete change in identity: the symbols by which the self is presented are replaced by the opposite. The tight miniskirt is replaced by long wide frocks, the thin nylons become dark stockings, the radiant smile a withdrawn face. Colour becomes gray or black. Extroversion and outgoingness become introversion and seclusion. Secularism is replaced by religiosity. But is it indeed such a radical change of identity for the women involved as it looks from the outside? How do women themselves perceive this change? To what extent does this new self, or the presentation thereof, conflict with the old self? Why do they construct such new identities?

In this chapter I will look at the shifting notions of self of Aisha and other women and how their multiple identities continually contest each other. Gender is an important element in Islamist or nationalist identity politics. Gender is also an important identity element by itself, in how women define themselves as women. How women combine (or struggle with) their different identities is essential in understanding women's participation in Islamist movements. The main aim of this article is to show how women use Islam as a stock of symbols, signs and signals, not only to change their religious identity, but even more so their personal identity in relation to their most significant others.

Notions of Identity

The concept of identity is at present in flux. Josselson (1990: 12-13), a psychologist interested in identity formation amongst women, wrote:

> In psychodynamic terms, identity is neither a structure nor a context but a property of the ego that organizes experiences. It is an amalgam, according to Erikson, of constitutional givens, idiosyncratic libidinal needs, psychological defenses against inner conflict, significant identifications with important others, interests and social roles. In a sense, we might think of identity formation as the assembling of a jigsaw puzzle in which each person has somewhat different pieces to fit together.

She is quite confident that most people will manage to put the jigsaw puzzle together and have a sense both of internal coherence and meaningful relatedness to the real world. She describes in her books several examples of how women 'have found themselves'.

Others have disputed this notion of identity as a sense of self and of wholeness that can be 'found', as if it were a construct that is 'there'. They rather present a picture of identity as something that is continually in construction, a puzzle that is never finished and always mixed up with other puzzles. For instance Judith Butler (1990: 25) said: 'There is no gender identity behind the expressions of gender; ... identity is performatively constituted by the very "expressions" that are said to be its results.' Identity cannot be found but only created in an ongoing process within specific power constellations. Butler therefore demands that students of identity investigate 'the political stakes in designating as an *origin* and *cause* those identity categories that are in fact the *effects* of institutions, practices, discourses with multiple and diffuse points of origin' (ibid.: ix) In other words, for women gender as an identity category is not caused by her sex, but the result of the complex interaction between women and the persons, institutions, symbols and power structures around her.

Contradictions in identity arise because people belong to different groups in relation to which they develop a social identity at the same time (Tajfel 1978, 1982; Skevington & Baker 1989). These groups, and the person's position in them, make conflicting demands on the individual. Women especially are confronted with conflicting identities imposed on them. First, because they more often belong to the less powerful groups and so have less influence on the models of femaleness being imposed on them, and on the representations of themselves as subjects. Secondly, because certain combinations, such as being a caring parent and a professional, remain inherently problematic (Roland 1979) and seem to be more of a problem for women than for men.

Moreover, the impact of each group — be it the family, the religious community, ethnic group, peer group, or work environment — shifts over time in conjunction with the lifecourse of the individual. Family relations and connections with the home become stronger when a woman marries and has children, while relations with friends tend to lessen. The self is continually and rapidly shifting as Ewing has shown in her seminal article 'The

Illusion of Wholeness: Culture, Self and the Experience of Inconsistency' (1990). She argued that people give plural, inconsistent self-representations which are context dependent. At different times and in interaction with different people, a different aspect of the self comes to the fore, and a different element of one's identity is presented. Nevertheless, people experience them as one, often fail to see how they are changing, and prefer to think that the contradictions are or should be resolved. This idea finds its parallel in the Foucaultian concept of the dispersed subject, which states that people's identity is constituted through subject positions set up in discourses which are specific to place and time in history. This process largely occurs unconsciously and does not prevent people from feeling a sense of wholeness. Moreover, it is not restricted to non-Western cultures, which are supposedly more contextual and relational, but a universal semiotic process (ibid.: 251).

On a cultural level the illusion of wholeness is constructed by symbolic means. Clothes, rituals, or behaviourial rules, which may include rules on such diverse areas as food-taboos, greeting forms, body posture, or use of machines or public space, give a sense of continuity and constancy to identities. They serve to identify those who belong and to differentiate them from those who do not belong. For the participants themselves, it heightens the awareness of who they are, and creates a sense of belonging and difference from others (Cohen 1995: 53). This is all the more urgent under conditions of intense political, economic or religious conflicts in the wider society. Shifts in identity on the individual level then intertwine with shifts in collective identities. The wider context influences the form and the content of the symbolic expression of the different elements of the self and the speed with which these change. The overt and visible choices of symbols by individuals may give an indication of the reconciliation of the demands of the various levels on the individual, but only partly and temporarily so. Observers tend to read a more constant and fixed identity out of the use of these symbols than is intended by the users. When women start to use an Islamist veil and thus emphasize one type of identity (religious), do they perceive themselves as having acquired an Islamist identity which contests their previous religious identity? And how do they reconcile this with their other identities as secretary, mother, daughter, video-assistant or designer of high-tech factories. How do they recreate the illusion of wholeness under these new conditions?

Shifting Boundaries between Self and Group

The question is to what extent the symbol of veiling really stands for a change in identity, and specifically in which identity. Asad urges us to unpack 'the comprehensive concept which he or she translates as "religion" into heterogeneous elements' (1993: 54). Part of this is, in my view, to see the new veiling not as a strictly religious symbol, but to show how it is intimately linked to social life and power relations therein. If it is strictly seen as a religious phenomenon it may be explained as only a communication of a profound change in private religious beliefs rather than also of other changes in social life and one's identity. As the questions of Aisha show, she was more involved with the symbols of her religion than with doubts about her beliefs. For her, her beliefs did not change; what was more significant was the way she would from now on express them, and take them seriously. After having settled down as a homemaker and mother of two children, she wants to be respected as such. Although she did not pray regularly and because of her pregnancies was not very serious about keeping the fast, she does not consider her plans to pray and fast more regularly now, as a change in belief. On the contrary, it is more a confirmation of the beliefs that were always there. When she uses Koranic citations now in discussions with her husband, she refreshes her memory of things learned long ago, rather than applying a totally new discourse. Women like Aisha have always considered themselves Muslims. Only they used to be young and careless and not yet serious. Their new religious practices form more of a confirmation of what they already were and what they believed but never showed, than a totally new religious identity.

The large variety in the degree and form of female veiling reflects the variation in the alternative modes of self-image. Of the growing group of modern veiled women that wear 'Islamic dress', only a small minority experience a profound shift in religious identity. The distinction between the days of ignorance, before they became religious, and the days of *hidaya* or the current situation, is very important for these radical fundamentalists. They are far stricter in their practices, for instance in their relations with non-related men or non-Muslims. The types of veiling they adopt reflect their attitude: they use gloves, completely cover their face with a *niqab*, and preferably wear dark colours. Religion is a major preoccupation in their lives, and they are somewhat impatient and scornful with the fad followers who choose daring colours and styles or who make only half-hearted attempts to discover the merits of a more religious life.

A larger group of women is far less sure what is the proper way. By asking others' advice about how to express what is already there, Aisha seeks to align herself to the moral consensus of the religious group and thus make the boundary between herself and the religious environment more permeable and her identity more defined through them. Let me compare Aisha's case with that of Nawal, a young Algerian woman who also took to the veil, because there are some striking similarities. Despite the socio-economic and political differences between Jordan and Algeria, resulting in a much larger adherence to fundamentalist movements in Algeria, on the personal level the experiences of the women seem to have much in common. When I met Nawal in 1981 she was an unmarried Algerian career woman who had studied law and then occupied a top position at a large state firm in one of the larger towns in Western Algeria. She lived in a villa provided by the firm, dressed in smart suits, and was regularly driven by one of the chauffeurs to the headquarters in Algiers for a meeting. Nawal considered herself a good Muslim, kept the fast, but did not pray regularly. Ten years later she was married, had three children and had quit her job (in that order). She prayed five times a day, did not leave the house without her husband's permission, and veiled herself. When we discussed her plans to take on the veil in 1984, she said it made her happy to be able to clarify her identity in that way. Just like Aisha she did not consider it a change in beliefs but rather an intensification and explication of them. She had always considered herself an outsider in the community because of her exceptional way of living, but now she felt 'back home' again. Aisha and Nawal now both define their self more through the religious community, but one of the consequences of this is that their identity has become more differentiated from that of another group: the family.

Cultures differ in the way the boundary between self and others is drawn, and thus in the measure of autonomy accorded to individual identity, as well as in who are the significant others. In Jordan the most significant others were always family, and individual identity was and still is strongly defined by family relations. This was illustrated by the reaction of a Jordanian student to whom I gave a low grade for an exam paper. He said: 'I can't get an F because I belong to the (tribe of) M's.' At that time I did not yet grasp the meaning of this remark, only that he considered it a strong argument in his effort to make me raise his mark. Jordan is still very much a tribal society in which tribes are hierarchically ordered and vying for power through control of its individual members. Family ties and the power of the family name can be decisive in getting a partner, a job, entrance to the university and even in getting good grades. In the student's view, his grades should match his family's status, rather than his personal ability. Moreover, he used his tribe's high rank and power as a threat to his teacher, which, if the teacher had been Jordanian and more sensitive and obedient to local power hierarchies instead of a foreigner who did not know who the M's were, might have had some effect.

Another example of the hold of family over the individual, and of the predominance of family identity over individual identity, can be found in the family associations (*jama'iyya*). The main goal of such associations is to enable regular contact between family members, for instance by providing facilities for family gatherings, usually in the form of a guest house which is used for weddings, circumcision feasts, or the parties of the unmarried males. The family associations also function as insurance- and saving-funds. Some have special arrangements to save for the education of the children, others provide loans to members and/or provide mutual support at death. The strong social control this leads to is exemplified by the case in which a young man found the guesthouse of his family closed on the day of his wedding. He had reserved the hall for his wedding party, but his cousin had locked the door and taken the key to protest that the groom had not shown sufficient familial respect. He had planned a wedding while his clan was still in mourning for an aunt who had died two months before, and moreover he had preferred to marry a 'stranger' rather than one of his cousins.

Women's boundaries of self are considered to be more permeable than men's in many cultures. This is expressed by the term 'relatedness'. Josselson (1987: 175) says that the process of anchoring is critical to the process of identity formation of women because the self is experienced so much in relation to others. She distinguishes four areas in which anchoring takes place: primary family, husband/children, career, friends. In this anchoring women may differ from men. Women are for instance less tied to a career and more tied to their children, as a result of which loss of a job will be less likely to lead to an identity crisis. Women's identity is therefore more marked by relatedness; as Josselson says identity is not a matter of being but fundamentally of being *with*.[3]

A similar phenomenon can be noticed in Jordan where women's identity depends even more on the family than men's identity. The naming system is very much indicative of this. Small children are often called by the term they will later have to address the speaker with, and thus made aware of the proper family relation. A girl might thus be called *'ammi* (lit. 'my uncle') by her father's brother, and *khâlti* (lit. 'my aunt') by her mother's sister.[4] People in general are often identified by their family relation, as father or mother of someone, or daughter of so and so. But this is far more often the case for women than for men. A woman is seldom called by her first name, but rather as *'bint-*X', daughter of X, before marriage, *'â'ilat-*Y', family of Y, after marriage, and *'umm-*Z', mother of Z, after the birth of her son.[5] These words anchor women to others and express their relatedness to relevant others to the point of ignoring their individual identity. The name symbolizes that a woman's choices are the choices of others. Before marriage X will decide how she dresses, where she goes and whom, when and where she marries. When the father is replaced by the husband, Y will decide when and where she goes or whom she shall see, and when both father and husband have died, Z will take over and decide how and where his mother will live. Female obedience is especially required in the field of sexuality and modesty. All control over their sexuality and any references to it have to be put in the control of men. Men are urged to impose this control by sayings like: *'Hamm al-bnât* *lemma mât'* (Protect the girls until death). Since *hamm* also means anxiety or concern, the underlying notion is that a father will be troubled by the presence of his daughter until she dies. The names by which a woman is called express a deep-felt conviction that a woman's identity is subsumed under that of the family group. The total subordination of her own identity to that of her family is a symbol of the strength of the group, her modest behaviour a symbol of the family's status and honour.

The transfer of authority from the father to the husband, however, is the first weak point in the ideology that denies an autonomous self to women. Whose authority is decisive, that of the father or the husband? Moreover, in practice, women as living actors are not always able or willing to conform completely with the orders of the males of the family. An example can be found in the case of 26-year old Jordanian Amina who wanted a divorce. Dissatisfied with her second husband, who locked her up in the house, she ran home. Her brother brought her back and tried to reconcile the couple, but as soon as she could she ran home again. Then her husband accused her of adultery (in an effort to avoid the obligation to pay a *mahr muta'akhkhira*), to which her father and brother reacted vehemently. It meant a blemish on their honour and they tried to convince the husband that if his wife was adulterous it was his fault and he was to blame and not her parents. The father negotiated a divorce having as the main argument not that his daughter was unhappy or the marriage not working, but that the husband was unable to command her obedience. Meanwhile her eldest brother blamed her father and her husband for not listening earlier to his warnings that the young man would have difficulties in controlling such an experienced woman with children. The subject of the discussion, Amina, withdrew and did not talk with them, but in the meantime had her own way, while the men contested each other's authority and inability to effect it.[6]

The norms of obedience are often far removed from reality. Formerly women had to leave home to fetch water from the well and wild herbs from the field, or help herd the goats or bring in the wheat harvest. Now an increasing number of women find work in schools, offices, and institutions. Both Zohra, my 48-year-old neighbour, and Mûna, her 20-year old daughter, were and are often out of sight and away from the authority of the responsible male. Zohra recounted how hard she had to work since she was eleven years old, after her mother had died and she had to take over her mother's share of the land labour as well as the housework for a father, six brothers and a mentally ill sister. She did everything, mowed, reaped, bound up the sheaves of wheat and winnowed, she ground the grain by hand, kneaded the dough and baked the bread in a self-made furnace. Life was difficult then and the father's permission for her activities out of doors was taken for granted rather than asked. Her daughter, who was born on the land during the harvest, studied to become a licensed nurse and recently found employment in a hospital in the next town. Mûna is formally engaged to a bus driver whom she met on the bus to school. He encourages her to work to save for her trousseau and their new apartment to be built on top of his father's house. Her independence is not very compatible with the ideal of complete obedience and she suffers from the results of this inconsistency. On the one hand she holds a responsible job where she often has to work at night and regularly comes into contact with unrelated men, on the other hand she is scolded by her fiancé for walking unchaperoned from his parents to her parents' house (about 300 metres). She has to copy him in presenting their marriage as an arranged one, in line with the ideal, instead of giving the romantic version that they fell in love on the bus. In short, the norms of female obedience are still vivid, and there are many efforts to enforce them, but women resist being moulded even more than before.

The ideal of women's identity as being dissolved in the identity of the family group includes her religious identity. Her religious behaviour and belief is supposedly made subject to male parental approval. Antoun, who described the religious lessons by which Jordanian Muslims were made familiar with Islamic ethics, paraphrases one preacher who said in 1960: 'A woman may not undertake a voluntary supererogatory fast without first seeking the permission of her husband. The purpose of this rule is not to discourage fasting but to stress the necessity of the obedience of the wife' (Antoun 1993: 616). He voices an ideal that to a large extent is still upheld today. The incorporation of woman's religious identity under that of her family is expressed by the

saying 'a woman follows her husband', which means that upon
marriage a woman takes her husband's religion. The imperative
for women to obey the husband is larger than the imperative to be
a believer. This idea is the basis for the Islamic rule that Muslim
men can marry a non-Muslim woman, as this leads to an increase
in Muslims, but a Muslim woman cannot marry a non-Muslim
man, as she would lose her religion.[7] That the woman is not
treated as an independent agent is further corroborated by the
statement than when this happens, it would be her father who is
to blame for her apostasy as he arranged her marriage.

Men's control over women's religious identity even extends
into the hereafter. Jordanian women told of their conviction that
upon the death of a woman her husband can veto her entrance to
heaven by not forgiving her for being angry with him, even if it
was his fault.[8] Some women however believe that this gendered
fate is not absolute, and that age or parental authority can give
them a similar right. During a discussion on a decorative wall
hanging with the maxim: 'Heaven is under the feet of the
mothers', one woman explained that women can earn heaven by
bringing up their children well and that they can also decide on
whether their sons go to heaven. A son who is not forgiven by his
mother will never go to heaven. The religious identity of social
minors, a status which women keep during most of their life, is
decided by their family. This control of the family over a
woman's religious identity illustrates that the kin group tries to be
more influential than the religious group, and to make kin identity
more important than religious identity.

During the last twenty years, however, the lines between
individuals and their family have been redrawn and made clearer,
and previous loyalties have been questioned. The power of
families over the religious identity of their members is waning.
Female actors always tried to balance the different identities
according to the circumstances. New is the use of Islam by
women. First, they claim a more autonomous religious identity,
the reasons for which I will show further on. Secondly, by
claiming religious responsibility, they defy male parental control
in more than the religious domain, and protest against hierarchies
within the family. Drawing upon Islam a generation gap is

(re)created. Women are creating a niche to make their own decisions by playing out the different loyalties.

To obtain a change in their position, women historically have used several of the identity strategies identified by Skevington and Baker (1989) and Tajfel (1978). The first is *assimilation* which involves the adoption of the positive features of the high-status group by the low-status group who wish to join them. The second is social *creativity* whereby the subordinate group seeks to create a new and positive image for itself through new symbols, language, history and so on or through the reinterpretation of negative features. The last is social *competition* when the subordinate group challenges the basis of the status hierarchy and seeks to change the relative power and status of groups by active or passive resistance.

There are theoretical limits to this political project, such as the claim of a collective identity based on gender for such a diverse group which is internally divided by lines of class, colour, or nationality, or the danger of an essentialist notion of gender identity, which feminists would want to avoid, but which Islamists use to their advantage. The different perspectives of the participants, their historical and hierarchical relations, as well as the cultural symbols and rituals used, must be taken into account. This is easier to do if we start with certain individuals in specific contexts. Despite these warnings, all three strategies can be recognized in the identity politics of women Islamists.

Islamism as an Identity Strategy for Women

The Moroccan sociologist Fatima Mernissi calls Islamic fundamentalism a 'statement about identity' (1987: 5). For both young men and women it is a protest against established economic, political, religious and moral hierarchies. When identity organizes experiences, as Josselson (1987: 12) states, it must be asked which experiences have to be dealt with. In the literature on the Islamic revival the influence of the economic and political crisis has been frequently discussed (Wagtendonk & Aarts 1986; Antoun 1993; Marty & Appleby 1993; Zebiri 1993). A dominant picture in the literature on 'fundamentalism', especially by its critics, is that 'the people' (read 'men') are in crisis, due to economic, political and moral chaos, that they adhere to 'fundamentalist' ideas in order to change the world. In their zeal to establish a new moral order they use 'the modest woman' as a symbol and force real women of flesh and blood to retreat to the home. In this picture, compulsory veiling is analyzed as a mechanism of social control of women, and 'symbolizes the lack of choice in the selection of identity: identity in the form of *hijab* is imposed' (Moghadam 1993: 143). But this bombardment of women with their normative identity is only one side of the matter. Not only is the male offensive not as effective as often supposed,[9] it also leaves out the role of women.

A subdominant picture is provided by studies which start out from a woman's perspective (e.g. MacLeod 1991; Zuhur 1992) and try to answer the question why women adhere to fundamentalist notions. Women not only respond to Islamist movements and adapt their identity accordingly, they actively take part in these movements, and use Islam, just like men, to shape their identity. Outside observers may not like that in doing so these women take over the idiom of their oppressors and limit their freedom of dress and movement, simplify reality and exalt their domestic activities. But portraying them as vulnerable victims of an objectionable ideology is a missed chance for understanding the rise of Islamism and the meaning of Islam for women's identity. It is also an unsatisfactory answer to my wondering why Aisha and Nawal suddenly decided to become serious, given the fact that none of their families nor their immediate surroundings tried to push them in that direction. Aisha's own parents let their daughters decide for themselves what to wear. Nor did her in-laws insist on Islamist dress or behaviour; her mother-in-law, who did not veil, had often extolled my decent dress when we were visiting, thereby implicitly commenting on the much shorter skirts of her daughter-in-law. But decent dress for her did not necessarily mean Islamic dress. She scolded her own eldest married daughter once that she could better prove herself as a good Muslim by helping her parents rather than by covering her head with a veil. Nawal's mother never abandoned her traditional Algerian *haik*, but never expected her daughters to veil, whether they were married or not. She even complained when one of her daughters was forced to veil by her in-laws. Neither Aisha nor Nawal felt that an identity was forced on them, but rather that they were expressing their own selves, and subsequently impressing these identities on their husbands.

To explain the appeal of Islamist movements among university and educated women, it is important to show that not only the boys are in crisis, but that the girls are even more so. Women who actively become Islamiyya seemed until a few years ago still comfortable in school or at work, and not afraid to use public space. Their life at that time seemed far removed from that of their mothers, who were hardly literate and who probably had moved from the countryside into town. Their fathers were still associated with low status jobs like agricultural or industrial worker and their mothers kept full seclusion and veiling whenever they could afford it in this urban environment (cf. also Ahmed 1992: 222; Zuhur 1992: 63). The young unmarried daughters saw themselves as different from their mothers. They had moved up a few social steps and learned the latest Wordperfect program on the computer rather than how to spin wool. They sat on chairs rather than sheepskins, walked outside with friends rather than remaining secluded, and worked in a bank or office rather than in the kitchen. But this difference put a heavy strain on these young girls. The gap with the milieu of the mother was acutely felt, moreover their dealing with the modern world was filled with frustrations.

Just like the boys, the girls could not cope with the economic situation. Economic changes led an increasing number of women like Aisha and Nawal to follow an education, seek paid employment and aim for the symbols of independence: an income, Western clothes, freedom of movement, mobility — maybe even a car — and decision-making power in economic matters. But they were frustrated on two fronts: due to the economic malaise it soon became difficult to obtain the coveted material goods. Higher education no longer brought the high gains promised, although the modern amenities and luxuries kept staring down at them from billboards, and were flashed at them by the conspicuously consuming elite, and by soaps and commercials on television.

Moreover, even when gained, the new freedoms proved to conflict very much with the traditional identity of daughter and wife. The family relentlessly demanded familial loyalty and obedience. As in the case of Mûna's fiancé, they kept imposing norms which could not be combined with the exigencies of paid work. A young university professor complained that at work she is responsible for a whole department, its students and curriculum, that she studied in America and drives everywhere in her car; but that at home her father expects her to take the man he chooses and to leave all her property behind when she marries, and her brothers expect to be served whenever they see fit and ask her to account for every step she takes and every person she talks to. In her daily contacts she has to fight for respect, because she is a women and people doubt her sexual mores. The wider society does not accept the take-over of the public space by schoolgoing girls and working women.

Especially Nawal felt this non-acceptance acutely. Living in a provincial town she had felt quite unhappy because she was not married yet, and people gossiped about her independent living. It was particularly difficult to maintain a measure of authority over her male subordinates. Women who adopted features of the higher-status males such as education, public space, careers, political office, smoking and driving, challenged the basis of the gender hierarchy. They became competitors with men for power resources. Men who saw their authority and dominance dwindling, could find in Islamist ideology the terms and the arguments to strike back. Drawing on the traditional equation of spatial boundaries with sexual boundaries, women's coming out of the home was seen as a loss of sexual control. And the reaction was in that same line: strict sexual mores had to be re-established by stricter rules for the use of public space for women and by regulating the public visibility of women's bodies.[10] At first sight, women increasingly seem to yield to this pressure, but many of them do so in a subversive way. Young women who feel frustrated with the future and with the past, solve it by creating an alternative image of women and themselves which is neither the image of a Western woman nor the image of their mother. The first symbolizes a separateness and loneliness they do not aspire to and the second implies a relatedness and obedience they want to escape.

In women's use of Islam, the three above-mentioned strategies can be discerned. By veiling, women partly assimilate to this dominant normative model. They retake established ways to gain respect: veiling, modest behaviour, segregation of the sexes. They also seem assimilated in the use of the respected source-books, the Koran and the Hadith, and the use of fragments of one's personal and collective history to create an identity. They study the sources and write history, for instance the life stories of Muhammad's wives, to serve as role models for present-day women.

More important however is social creativity, the second strategy in identity politics. For although old symbols and histories are used, they are put in a different form to create a different identity. The veil of the new Islamists is very different from that of their mothers. The change in form betrays a significant change in meaning and in the women underneath. The new veil no longer refers to the respectful women secluded in the home, as previously, but rather to the young career women, working in offices and travel agencies. The *hijab* (a long sober overdress with a large headscarf) of the latter is more practical, international, sober, and uniform. By updating and upgrading an old symbol, young women have sought to create a new and positive image for themselves, features previously considered negative have been reinterpreted, loyalty to a larger, even international, Islamic community has been expressed.

The creation of a new identity to show to outsiders is an arduous and long process. Women seldom turn Islamist overnight. Aisha decided to wear long clothing and go veiled a few weeks before Ramadan, the Holy Month which usually releases more religious sentiments. But she postponed taking action. She would say: 'Tomorrow I will do it,' while she put on her finest city clothes, did her face in full colours and went shopping in town. Her sister-in-law encouraged her by giving her a beautiful black shawl embroidered with hundreds of bright little flowers. She wore that for a while and clearly loved it. She kept saying: 'Isn't it pretty?'. I nodded, and bit back the remark at the tip of my tongue that veiling is not meant to make a woman prettier but rather less appealing. Instead I teased her by saying that now she might not be able to wear that pretty winter suit she had just bought. She said she would put on boots with that so that her legs were covered. Her traditional embroidered dress, a present from her mother for her trousseau but never worn, was recovered from the bottom of a trunk and let out. In the first week of Ramadan she went with her husband to an Islamist store to order an overgown, grumbled about the drab colours, and realized her previous choices had been too fancy and bright. With a sigh, she hid the pretty shawl in a drawer and also the embroidered dress returned to the trunk.

Many young women in Jordan and other countries go through a similar process. A comparison of the pictures in the *Yearbooks* of Yarmouk University illustrate the gradual increase in veiling. In 1980 of the female graduates 17 per cent were veiled, in 1986 this figure had risen to 39 per cent and three years later, in 1986, it reached 47 per cent.[11] Many students are pragmatic about it. One student told me: 'My father hesitated to let me study, but my taking on the veil brought him around,' and another: 'At least now we do not get bothered so much by the male students.'

Finding the right symbols, and through them working on a new religious identity, happens in the continuous interaction of the individual with her surroundings. On the way, the most obvious conflicts with other loyalties and sides of one's identity must be solved. The new veil, unlike most of the traditional veils of Jordanian and Algerian women, is 'workable' as it allows economic activity. Unlike the Algerian *haik*, which had to be pressed against the body by the two upper arms and needed to be held with one hand before the face, the new veil leaves both hands ready to work, the eyes open to see and the mouth visible and audible. Moreover, the new veil expresses transnational anti-Western sentiments in its international uniformity. The image of the young veiled woman behind the computer is part of national pride.

Paradoxically, the greater conformity with and dependence on the wider religious community and the search for moral consensus is used by people to take individual choices and be personally responsible. This obligation in the religious domain to be accountable for oneself and to be individually responsible for realizing Islamic values, has effects on the social domain where individual responsibility and accountability are also claimed by women with the help of religious arguments. Here the third strategy of identity politics comes to the fore: social competition whereby the subordinate group challenges the basis of the status hierarchy and seeks to change the power balance.

Threatening the Cohesion of the Family: Widening the Generation and Gender Gap

In their creative strategy, young Islamist women may on the one hand seem to return to old symbols and bow to the generation of their parents, but on the other hand, by adopting a dress which is more international, sober, practical and uniform, and by adhering to ritual rigidity and a strict avoidance between the sexes, they react to and challenge old hierarchies.

Many women who turn more visibly to Islam take this decision themselves: the family does not impose this identity, although they cannot easily disapprove. Aisha is convinced that it is her own decision. When I asked what her husband thought about it, she answered: 'He said: you have to decide for yourself.' In reality, when she announced her decision to her husband, he said: 'That is better.' and then, turning to me as if defending her: 'Everybody thinks that is better. In our religion one has to dress *shara'i.*'[12] It was the first time however that I heard him say something positive about it, as he usually found her very attractive in her Western clothes and never gave any hint that he wanted her to change, nor did he have any tendency himself to adhere to new rules. When I asked for a reason, Aisha recounted how a week earlier she had walked to her mother-in-law in a short skirt and the neighbours had climbed to the roof to look at her. During her visit she had felt upset, because the skirt was too tight on her as she had not yet regained her figure after her last pregnancy, and it kept creeping up. Moreover, it cost too much money to buy nylons all the time. She would gain more respect and dress more cheaply in Islamic dress. Aisha felt she had to excuse her choice. Not that she expected disapproval, but neither had her husband, his family or her circle of friends suggested anything in that direction. On the contrary, she had little direct contact with other Islamists, nor would she call herself an Islamist.

Some respected members of the older generation tried to discourage her and reacted with irritation at the young woman's zeal. When Aisha, dressed in her recently acquired Islamic outfit, visited her husband's great-aunt, the old lady reacted both to her veiling and my presence, by telling the following joke, warning us beforehand that it was 'not religious'. She said (I paraphrase her):

It deals with the three important prophets. God said to the first, Moses: Go and select your people. And Moses looked over the people and selected from them the most beautiful women. Later came Jesus, and God said to him: Go and select your people. And Jesus went and selected the most beautiful women. When it was the third prophet's turn and God told him to select his people, there were only ugly women left, with wry faces and crooked arms. So Mohammad said: 'Cover your faces and follow me.'

Aisha did not smile, neither did I, as I was somewhat embarrassed about this Orientalist joke. Yet it made clear the old lady's objection to and distaste of veiling. Depending on their socio-economic background and their personal convictions, not all mothers react in the same way to their daughters' new veiling. In Egypt, some mothers had struggled themselves to come out of seclusion and considered the removal of the veil liberating; 'they are unhappy to see their daughters "undoing" their gains' (Rugh 1993: 163). In Algeria, where the process of giving up the veil by the mothers' generation was stopped during the Algerian revolution as the veil became a symbol of resistance against the French, it was more common to find veiled women who preferred their daughters to go unveiled, as in the case of Nawal's mother. Although they themselves kept the conservative *haik*, they wished for their daughters the liberty they fought for but never got. Nawal's mother was disappointed about the changes and would often sigh: 'We fought the war of independence for nothing.' The situation found by Rugh in Egypt, that mothers sometimes donned modern Islamic dress at the urging of their daughters, is seldom found in Algeria because a larger percentage of women still wear the traditional veil.

Despite these critiques, however, people cannot easily disapprove the striving for a better moral life. They might think it overdone, or not timely for a young woman who does not yet have to think about her afterlife, or not necessary for being a good Muslim, but parents, husband and other relatives cannot deny a young woman responsibility for her own deeds because she herself will be held accountable. Islamists hold each person responsible for her or his own salvation, and not only the family patriarch. They know Sura 4: 84, 'Therefore fight for the cause of God. You are accountable for none but yourself. Rouse the faithful: perchance God will overthrow the might of the unbelievers. God is mightier and more truculent than they.' (Koran, interpr. Dawood). Also women are required to make their own religious decisions, even if this implies that they contradict and disobey their father or husband. When negotiating their religious autonomy and a new power position, women often use the expression: 'No one should obey a created being in the disobedience of the Creator' (*la ta'at li-makluq fi ma'siyat al-Kaliq*) from the Hadith. Many women have discovered in Islam a strategy for increasing their decision-making power. When relatives refuse her this right, she will tell them her rights with the holy scriptures in hand.

This new-found autonomy is repeated in other domains. Aisha took to the veil during a turbulent time in her marriage. She had supported her husband in his proposal to buy a piece of land, yet without her knowing he had used her money but had not put the land in her name too. For weeks she was angry, refusing to cook for him and sleep with him. Wearing the new symbol made her confident in her beliefs and religious knowledge, so she started to quote Koranic verses to show that he was a bad Muslim because he had stolen her bridewealth and property. He could not but repent his wrongdoing. Peace returned to the household when he promised to have the property deeds written in the name of their two daughters. She announced she would go back to work again in order to refill her bank-account, and he better not dare say that it was improper for a mother to work because she was wearing Islamic dress and thus proved her modesty. It is significant that in using her religious knowledge to influence her relation with her husband she felt less insecure and did not ask others for advice. Nawal in Algeria also used religious knowledge in her arguments with her husband. He had started drinking and maltreating her at the time and by slowly interesting him in a more religious life she worked to improve his behaviour.

Not only the line between women and their husbands but also between girls and their fathers is redrawn. By turning Islamist they challenge the kinship hierarchy as well as the gender hierarchy. To use terms like 'sisters and brothers' for religious peers appears an assimilation to kinship values. But their implication of equality between women and men as believers defies the patriarchal ordering of women and men as daughters and fathers. Young women can find in Islamist ideologies legitimate excuses to defy the father's choice of marriage partner when the proposed groom does not show sufficient religious zeal. The fundamentalist group will support them in arguing that religious loyalty is more important than loyalty to the family. Women use a religious idiom and religious symbols to defend their own choice to work, to use public space, to marry, but also to criticize their fathers and husbands for not giving women their due rights, for refusing them an education or their own property, for using alcohol and drugs, or for spending their money on the street rather than on their family.[13] A widening gap is acutely felt by many families.

When the daughter or wife decides to follow her own rules for dress and behaviour instead of obeying her male kin, conflicts may arise, not only because they might disapprove, but also because it is one of the few areas where women openly make their own choices *and can defend them*. Moghadam quotes an account by Coffman who was fascinated by the way young girls reconciled their fundamentalist lifestyle with their dream of succeeding in thermodynamics and become civil engineers. They told him that nothing irritated them more than the efforts of many Algerian men to veil their women by force and abuse them into submission. 'I think it's scandalous how men dominate women in Algeria!' seethed Aicha as she mechanically pushed an errant lock of hair back under her *hijab*. 'Listen, if I'm able to take on the *hijab* against the wishes of my father, another woman is also able to decide *not* to wear it, despite the wishes of her father. No woman should let herself be intimidated by a slap, a whack of the belt, or blackmail. A woman must stand up for her rights' (Moghadam 1993: 150).

The conflicts become more serious when they also try to impose their new moral behaviour on other family members. Islamist women set an example, both for themselves and for other women, but their exemplary and proselytizing behaviour is not always appreciated. Family members may get fed up with being called 'culturally un-authentic', 'Western', 'degenerate' or 'blasphemous' (Karam 1993: 10; Zebiri 1993: 219) when they have been doing nothing more than they always did. Fathers and brothers do not like to see their authority contested by what 'the Imam has said'. This has led to an irreparable rift in many families. Thus, a renewed adherence to Islam may change both a woman's relation to her family of birth and to her family of marriage. Family and religious peer group are contesting each other's influence on women's identity. This contest and the slow movement from the family to the religious community as primary identity group leaves room for the development of her own individual identity. Her autonomy versus the family increases. This diminishes the hold of men over female relatives. Andrea Rugh noted the same reshaping of personal relations in Egypt, where youngsters defy the father in the name of Islam, and girls can for instance refuse the father's choice of marriage partner with the argument that the boy is not a good Muslim. Rugh states: 'Religious movements are uniquely equipped in this respect to redefine personal loyalties toward the higher entity of community without destroying the stability that comes from strong family institutions.' Although I agree with this transfer of loyalties, I doubt whether the stability of strong family institutions is left intact. Islamism is becoming a divisive element in many families.

It is the paradox of Islamic ideology, which places so much emphasis on family cohesion and hierarchy, that it is used by women to undermine the authority of the father or husband. While reproducing the kinship tie in Islamic idiom, they defy the kinship and gender hierarchy.

Conclusion

Women's multiple identities are changing in a continuous interaction with wider social processes. The very visibility of the symbol of the veil suggests most changes in religious identity. I have tried to show in this chapter, however, that women's religious identity has not been radically changed. To the contrary; changes in their religious identity are not so much perceived as individual changes in belief system as in the ways these beliefs are expressed and turned into practice. Despite a new dress code and strict spacial and behaviourial rules, informants would deny a profound change in identity in this respect. What was put more into question was their familial identity. Resurgent religious groups demand loyalty to the *umma*, the religious community, over loyalty to the family and even over loyalty to male authority. Women were already contesting their relatedness and extreme subjugation to the family due to their increased autonomy in space, education or work. Dissatisfied with the past pattern according to which a woman's identity was subjugated to that of her family, and in which she only existed as daughter, wife or mother, but also frustrated with the Western model of women as career women, they applied social creativity as a strategy to mould old symbols, idiom and history into an identity that contained multitudes, and that was continually discussed and remade so that it could be experienced as one.

Let us take a last look at Aisha and Nawal. Both accommodated to the norms of the people they felt close to, but on their own terms. They did not take their mothers' veil or follow their mothers' secluded way of life, but took on a new veiling as both a symbol of religious autonomous responsibility as well as of their presence in the public domain. Both used it to protest against their husband. Veiling might also have been a form of protection against gossip about their relation with me, a non-Muslim and Western woman. Again it would make their 'real identity' clear to significant others. This decision to 'become serious' involved them in a complex decision-making process. They had to answer questions they never had to answer before and they had to rely on their own judgement as never before. They both used it also to request respect for their motherhood, Aisha for producing only girls, Nawal for liberating her from paid work when the combination of a full-time job with three small children became too strenuous. She convinced her husband to sell his car and take his duties as provider more seriously so that she could stop working.

Despite the very different national contexts in which Aisha and Nawal live, they show some similarities in the arguments they use to explain their choice and in the contextual elements that make such a choice understandable. Of course not all women have the same reasons for turning Islamist, nor share the same socio-economic background. The modern media, however, have helped to spread the discourse and the symbols that young women can draw from to orient themselves in this new endeavour. International exchange of information should not be underestimated in enabling women to formulate what they want in an Islamic idiom. It is on this level that women's Islamism from such widely divergent countries as Algeria and Jordan can be compared.

What does this mean for theory on fundamentalism? First, women have reasons for adhering to fundamentalist ideas and practices that are similar to men's, but they have also their own special reasons for adhering to fundamentalist ideas and practices. If we look at the literature on Islamist movements, and how this takes women and gender into consideration, we see that most of it departs from males as constituting the main body of Islamists. It has been argued here, however, that the growth of these movements cannot be understood properly without taking account also of women as a driving force behind them. If gender is mentioned, it is usually as an important issue in Islamist discourse, or in the context of the detrimental effects of Islamist movements on women. Neglected, however, is how women with the help of Islamist idiom construct their own gender identity which includes the right to study and to participate in the political and economic domains. Authors who describe the attractiveness of Islamism for women do so hesitantly, as they do not want to be considered apologists for an anti-rational, exclusive, potentially violent belief system. The problem lies in fundamentalism being both negative and positive for women, and in the importance of taking both sides into account.

Secondly, it was argued that when Islamist movements are interpreted as fundamental changes in religious identity the symbols are overrated. A visible change in the symbol of the veil does not necessarily imply a fundamental change in the belief system. Besides overrating the change in religious identity, this has as side effect that other identity changes, such as patrilineal or gender identity, are overlooked. Changing family and gender relations are both cause and effect of fundamentalism, and not only in negative ways.

Notes

1. The ethnographical data for this paper was gathered in a small town in Northern Jordan in 1989 and in a large provincial town in West Algeria in 1981-82 and 1984 (see respectively Jansen 1993b and Jansen 1987).

2. Critics of the concept of fundamentalism have pointed out its christiancentric, ethnocentric, homogenizing, demonizing and a-historical character (Esposito 1992: 8; Karam 1993: 4; Jansen 1993a: 32-3, n. 16). The alternative, 'Islamism', however, sounds less ethnocentric but suffers equally from the problem of suggesting homogeneity and a-historicity, can neither do justice to the differences and flux within Islamic movements, and suggests an objectivity which might not be there. The term fundamentalism on the other hand, enables fruitful comparisons between similar movements in different religions and points to many analogies in the centrality of gender in symbolism and ideology and in the effects on gender relations (Riesebrodt 1990; Hawley 1994). Moreover, there is nothing wrong in taking a critical stance as long as this is made explicit. These are valuable reasons why many continue to use the term 'fundamentalism' (as in Jansen 1993a; Hawley 1994; Marty & Appleby 1993). The main reason why I use the term Islamism alternating with, but more prominent than fundamentalism, is my anthropological tendency to use emic concepts wherever possible and relevant.

3. R. Josselson, lecture on Identity and Development, 27 September 1990 Amsterdam.

4. I would like to thank Farha Ghannam for her comment on this and other topics.

5. Only exceptionally is this order reversed. One legendary woman managed to have her son called after her instead of her being called after her son. Stories are told about her, that she took decisions like a man, talked at the well with the men, and composed poems like men. These stories show the potential breaks in the norms but at the same time serve to reinforce the general pattern.

6. The question of women's identity of daughter versus wife also returns in discussions on membership of family associations. In most associations women leave the one they belong to by birth for the one of their husband, at least for the financial aspects which now are arranged through the husband. But she and her husband will continue to be invited to the social gatherings twice a year of her clan of birth,

because, as they say: '*hiyya bintnâ*', she is our daughter. Establishing a woman's identity in these terms is essential for the claims on her obedience.

7. This last type of marriage is not legally possible in Jordan.

8. It is their personal interpretation of a widespread belief that believers upon their death must be pardoned for their faults by their co-religionists. The community of believers can thus decide if a person is to be saved.

9. The effect for instance on women's participation in the labour market is limited. Even in Iran women's average participation became not significantly lower after the revolution, although female judges and top officials lost their jobs, and many educated women fled the country (Moghadam 1988; Tabari 1986; Ramazani 1993).

10. In the manifesto of one of Algeria's Islamic parties, Al-Nahda ('revival'), part of the goal 'to spread virtuous morals and to defend them' is thought to be met by working for the abolition of mixing of the sexes in education, administration, health services and other work-places and establishments (Zebiri 1993: 215). Twenty years ago, in Algeria, an unveiled woman taking the bus, risked to be taken for a prostitute; today she risks being beaten on the legs, or worse, being killed.

11. Veiling is related to the discipline of study. Students in Biology, Physics, Mathematics, and Chemistry in particular wear veils (69 per cent of female graduates) and women studying Arabic (67 per cent), disciplines acceptable for girls under Islamic norms. Girls make up a large share of the student population in these disciplines. For example, in 1983/4 at Yarmouk University 31 per cent and at the University of Jordan 58 per cent of the students in the physical sciences were women. Veiled women can next be found in the English Department, probably for the opposite reason. In this case veiling prevents people from drawing false conclusions as to the girl's true loyalty when choosing this popular and prestigious discipline. Women in the Faculty of Economics and Administrative Sciences go largely unveiled, as do the few women in Sports, Journalism and Engineering.

12. The reader may wonder about my own views on this. I tried to remain neutral rather than approve or disapprove. However, in discussions my pronunciation was several times corrected from *shara'i* to *shara'i*, the first word means 'from the street' with the connotation of 'whorish', the latter 'according to the Shari'a, the Islamic law'. The letter 'ain in the second word is difficult to master for a foreign speaker, but not unfamiliar or unspeakable to me. Was this maybe a Freudian slip of the tongue?
13. For this protest character of the new veiling see also MacLeod 1991.

References

Ahmed, L. (1993), *Women and Gender in Islam*, New Haven & London: Yale University Press.

Antoun, R. (1993), 'Themes and Symbols in the Religious Lesson: A Jordanian Case Study,' *International Journal of Middle East Studies*, vol. 25, 607-24.

Asad, T. (1993), *Geneologies of Religion: Discipline and Reasons of Power in Christianity and Islam*, Baltimore & London: The Johns Hopkins University Press.

Botje, H. (1994), *Het duivelshuis*, Amsterdam: Prometheus.

Butler, J. (1990), *Gender Trouble. Feminism and the Subversion of Identity*, London: Routledge.

Cohen, A.P. (1995) (1st ed. 1985), *The Symbolic Construction of Community*, London: Routledge.

Esposito, J. L. (1992), *The Islamic Threat: Myth or Reality*, New York and Oxford: Oxford University Press.

Ewing, K.P. (1990), 'The Illusion of Wholeness: Culture, Self, and the Experience of Inconsistency', *Ethos,* vol. 18, no. 3, pp. 251-279.

Hawley, J.S. (1994), *Fundamentalism and Gender*, Oxford: Oxford U.P.

Jansen, W. (1987), *Women without Men. Gender and Marginality in an Algerian Town*, Leiden: E.J. Brill.

Jansen, W.(1993a), *Mythen van het fundament*, Nijmegen: SUN.

Jansen, W.(1993 b), 'Creating Identities. Gender, Religion and Women's Property in Jordan', in M. Brügmann et al. (eds),

Who's Afraid of Femininity? Questions of Identity, Amsterdam: Rodopi.

Josselson, R. (1990), *Finding Herself. Pathways to Identity Development in Women*, San Francisco: Jossey Bas.

Karam, A.M. (1993), *'Modernity' and Women's Groups in Egypt: Activist Women's Realities*, Amsterdam, (MERA Occasional Paper no. 20).

The Koran (1990) transl. by N.J. Dawood, London: Penguin.

MacLeod, A.E. (1991), *Accomodating Protest. Working Women, the New Veiling, and Change in Cairo*, New York: Columbia University Press.

Marty, M.E. & R.S. Appleby (eds) (1993), *Fundamentalisms and Society. Reclaiming the Sciences, the Family and Education*, Chicago/London: University of Chicago Press.

Mernissi, F. (1987), *The Fundamentalist Obsession with Women. A Current Articulation of Class Conflict in Modern Muslim Societies*, Lahore: Simorgh. Women's Resource and Publication Centre.

Moghadam, V. (1988), 'Women, Work and Ideology in the Islamic Republic', *International Journal of Middle East Studies*, vol. 20, no. 2, 221-43.

Moghadam, V. (1993), *Modernizing Women. Gender & Social Change in the Middle East,* Boulder: Lynne Rienner.

Ramazani, N. (1993), 'Women in Iran: The Revolutionary Ebb and Flow', *The Middle East Journal*, vol. 47, no. 3, 409-28.

Riesebrodt, M. (1990), *Fundamentalismus als patriarchalische Protestbewegung: Amerikanische Protestanten (1910-28) und iranische Shiiten (1967-79) im Vergleich*, Tubingen: J.C.B. Mohr (Paul Siebeck).

Roland, A. (1979), 'Identity as an Orienting Concept,' A. Roland & B. Harris (eds), *Career and Motherhood. Struggles for a New Identity,* New York: Human Sciences Press.

Roseman, M. (1990), 'Head, Heart, Ordor, and Shadow: The Structure of the Self, the Emotional World, and Ritual Performance among Senoi Temiar', *Ethos*, vol. 18, no. 3, 227-51.

Rugh, A. (1993), 'Reshaping Personal Relations in Egypt', in M.E. Marty & R.S. Appleby (eds), *Fundamentalisms and*

Society. Reclaiming the Sciences, the Family and Education, Chicago/London: University of Chicago Press.

Skevington, S. & D. Baker (eds) (1989), *The Social Identity of Women*, London: Sage.

Tabari, A. (1986), 'The Women's Movement in Iran: A Hopeful Prognosis', *Feminist Studies*, vol. 12, no. 2, 343-60.

Tajfel,H. (ed.) (1978), *Differentiation between Social Groups: Studies in the Social Psychology of Intergroup Relations*, London: Academic Press.

Tajfel, H. (1982), *Social Identity and Intergroup Relations*, Cambridge: Cambridge University Press.

Wagtendonk,K. & P. Aarts, (eds) (1986), *Islamitisch fundamentalisme*, Muiderberg: Coutinho.

Zebiri, K. (1993), 'Islamic Revival in Algeria: An Overview', *The Muslim World*, vol. 83, no. 3-4, 203-26.

Zuhur, S. (1992), *Revealing Reveiling. Islamist Gender Ideology in Contemporary Egypt*, Albany: State University of New York Press.

Chapter 4

Public Baths as Private Places

Marjo Buitelaar

In the film Halfaouine a Tunisian boy struggles to save the best of both worlds as he is bidding farewell to his childhood and taking his first steps towards adulthood. For boys in sex-segregated societies like the Maghreb-countries, growing up implies an irreversible transition from the world of women to the world of men. In Halfaouine, this transition results in a crisis when the boy accompanies his mother to the *hammâm* and is 'caught' peeping at one of the nearly naked women.

What I am interested in here is not so much the incident's symbolic marking of the protagonist's life-crisis, but the question why a boy's transgression should create such a state of frenzy among bathing women. There is not one single answer to this question. The public bath is a complex social situation which relates to many dimensions in women's lives.[1] In this article I will use the example of the public bath in Moroccan society to discuss the sexual division of space that is characteristic of North African cultures. The major part of the article consists of a description of the main features of the organization of social space and its correspondence to different notions of privacy. Next I will look into the paradox of the *hammâm* as the most private of public female domains. To a certain extent, the significance of this characteristic for women depends on their living arrangements, which both express and effect shifting notions of privacy. In the latter part of this chapter I will therefore investigate how modernization processes influence women's social relations and the differential importance of having access to female networks through the privacy of the *hammâm*.

The Concept of Privacy in Anthropology

It is common knowledge that social organization in Muslim countries in the Middle East is predominantly based on a sexual division of space. In accordance with the Islamic moral-legal code, men and women spend their daily lives in relatively separate spheres. Women's domains consist mainly of the house and the neighbourhood, while workplace, coffee shops, the market, the mosque and the street are typically men's domains. Schools form an interesting mixed domain, where more explicit male and female zones tend to arise among students as they get older.

Western educated anthropologists have easily been tempted to sum up such spatial arrangements by stating that women operate mostly within the private sphere and men in the public sphere. In the 1970s feminist researchers who were searching for grand theories to explain the universal subordination of women saw a causal relation between women's lack of power and what they perceived to be a greater preponderance of women in the domestic sphere and men in extra-domestic spheres. It was believed that women were nearly universally confined to the 'private' sphere, which prevented their access to authority, prestige and cultural values. These were thought to be the prerogatives of men, who competed for these sources of power in the 'public' sphere (cf. Rosaldo, 'Theoretical Overview' in *Women, Culture and Society*, 1974). This view was soon corrected by studies that showed that women could exert considerable informal power within the 'private' sphere and were also often able to influence decisions taken in the 'public' sphere through their husbands and sons.[2]

Since then, awareness has grown of the difficulty in assuming that the private-public dichotomy is a universal one, or that the criteria which determine what social situation people from varying cultures experience as 'private' or 'public' should be the same everywhere. Historians have pointed out that the Western interpretation of privacy as the right of a person to individual freedom and the conception of private and public spaces as mutually exclusive spheres are the result of slow historical developments (cf. Elias 1969 and Moore 1984). More recent ethnographic evidence suggests that in many cases private and public zones cannot be assessed by physical dimensions alone, but may be defined by sound and sight zones as well.[3] Public and private domains may be measured not only by space but by a wider context including time, participants and activities. In order to do justice to the different notions of privacy experienced by Moroccan women, I follow Sciama (Ardener 1981: 89) in defining privacy as the right or need of individuals or social groups to separate themselves from others at various times, or for certain well-defined activities.

Moroccan Notions of Privacy

A low level of spatial differentiation in traditional urban Moroccan houses and the remarkably mobile character of the furnishings confirm the contextual understanding of privacy suggested here above. Rooms tend to be of the same shape and size. Although the quality and decorations of furniture may differ from room to room, all rooms are basically furnished with the same *sdâris* or small divans that are arranged along the sides of the walls. When a family disposes over more than one room, the husband and wife may sleep in a double bed in one of the rooms, but otherwise there are no specific bedrooms. Even if a house consists of several rooms, most members of the family prefer to sleep together in one room, either on the *sdâris* or on thin mattresses that are laid out every night. In the morning the blankets and mattresses are put away again so that the room can be used for other purposes, such as entertaining guests and eating meals. The *mîda*, a small round table also moves around a lot. When the weather permits family members may prefer eating the main meal at midday in the courtyard, but the table is rolled back to one of the rooms for tea or to serve a guest of high status. A now vanishing custom is for husbands to eat apart. In most families, however, when there are no guests all family members eat together. Meals are served from a common plate.

These sleeping and eating arrangements illustrate the high value that Moroccans attach to sharing. Except maybe for the parents, hardly ever does an individual member of the family have a room or even a plate 'of one's own'. Indeed, the Western notion of privacy as the right of the individual to time or space for him- or herself is relatively weak and is socially depreciated.[4] Moroccans seldom withdraw themselves from company and such behaviour is met with suspicion. People who seek to be alone may either be thought to be ill, in which case they should be closely attended to, or they may be suspected to be up to some mischief, in which case the presence of others may prevent them from carrying out their plans.

A notion of privacy that is much more highly valued by Moroccans is family privacy, the right to hide family life from those who do not belong to the *qurâb* or 'close ones'.[5] The importance of family privacy can be recognized in the spatial organization of traditional Moroccan houses, which are turned inwards. Strangers easily get lost in the narrow, winding alleys that lead to the houses, so they stay away if they have no business there. The outside walls of the houses are high and if they have any windows at all, these tend to be very small, barred, and above eye-level so as to prevent passers by from peeping in. There is only one entrance to the house. The need to protect family life from the larger society can be illustrated by the fact that in cities in the Rif mountains in northern Morocco the front door is called *l-ltâm ad-dâr*, the veil of the house (Cammaert 1985: 81). Behind the low doorway is a small corridor that leads to the courtyard. The courtyard often lies a few steps below street level and the corridor may have bends. Again, this obstructs the view of what goes on inside. The courtyard is called *wust ad-dâr*, the centre of the house. The rooms around it can only be entered from the courtyard and catch light from windows in the walls facing it.

The place where guests are invited to sit down is an indication of the closeness between the visitor and the host family. While it is an honour for a special guest to be invited into the most luxuriously decorated room of the house, creating a temporary guest room is also a way of hiding the privacy of family life from view. On the rare occasion of men inviting male guests who are not close family the visitors are inevitably received in a 'guest room'. Women, on the contrary, only seldom receive their female guests in a special room. If the weather permits, close friends are invited to sit on the roof or in the courtyard. Otherwise female guests may be received in whatever room the hostess happened to be sitting at the moment of their arrival.

These gender differences illustrate that men are more concerned with family privacy than women. A man hardly ever invites his friends to his house. His domestic life is not their business.

Especially female members of the family should remain hidden from the outside world. Etiquette even forbids a relative stranger to the family to ask a man about his wife's health. A male acquaintance to the family will respect the family privacy by vaguely inquiring after *ad-dâr*, the house, meaning the members of the household.

Among women, family affairs are discussed more frequently and in more detail. Still, a female visitor does not readily mention the name of the husband of her hostess but is more likely to refer to him as *mûl ad-dâr*, the owner of the house. This is not only indicative of the power relations between the genders, but also points to the significance to women of gender privacy, the need and right of groups of the same gender to separate from persons from the other gender. By not mentioning his name, she distances herself from the husband of her friend.

As in many Muslim countries, the notion of gender privacy is a dominant ordering principle in the social organization and the corresponding spatial arrangements. In the company of other women, 'the brakes can be taken off certain impulses' as Moore (1984) describes the atmosphere of private groups to which individuals may temporarily retreat for protection and relief from the demands and obligations of larger society.

The house is associated with women's privacy to such an extent that it has developed feminine qualities itself. Walls are often painted in bright pink, blue or green colours that correspond with those of women's clothing. The divan covers usually have a flower design and, when money permits, contain brocade, likewise features that are exclusively reserved for women's clothing. Calling the front door 'the veil of the house' also illustrates an association of the house with the female body, which may also be protected by a veil against prying eyes. Combs-Schilling even goes as far as saying that the traditional Moroccan house is modelled on the female body.[6]

This is not to say that 'anything goes' for the women who meet within the intimate female privacy of a house. Depending on context, such relaxation can itself be highly stylized and imposes its own standards of behaviour.[7] This is especially the case in interaction with non-related women, in whose presence family privacy must also be protected to a certain extent. Of these two competing forms of privacy, gender privacy prevails, so that among themselves, women feel free to dress, sit, laugh, and talk in a way that they cannot do in the presence of men.

In the eyes of women, gender privacy can be more dominant than family privacy. Even in his own house, a man can be an unwelcome intruder when his wife is receiving guests. While his definition of the situation is that of a private place where family privacy prevails, in the view of his wife, and much more so in that of her friends, gender privacy is disturbed and the setting is transformed from a private place into a public one. In such cases, women cut off their conversation, check their posture and clothing, and expect the man to withdraw as quickly as possible.

In situations where this is not possible, as in the case of a woman who had no choice but to invite me into the same one-room dwelling where her ill husband lay on a divan, the two genders are likely to ignore each other. In this particular case, my hostess had to leave the room to fetch water to make coffee. In much the same way as Europeans in an elevator may choose to ignore the other occupants, her husband and I kept silent and evaded each other's glances. His presence was even more openly disregarded by his daughter who came in and greeted me, saying: 'What bad manners does my mother have to leave you sitting here all by yourself!'

Even when there are no visitors women may feel ill at ease when adult male members of the family are present. They feel checked in their activities and are on their guard not to discuss certain matters, particularly topics concerning sexuality. Teenage girls love to dance or sing along with the radio, but when their father or an older brother enters the house they stop at once and may be ordered by their mother to turn off the radio altogether. There is of course considerable variation between families. In liberal families gender privacy is not seldom overruled by family privacy and family members of both genders feel rather comfortable in the presence of each other. The attitude of more traditional women concerning mixed-gender domestic situations can perhaps best be illustrated by quoting a Moroccan proverb according to which 'A man about the house is like a boil on the back' — that is, a nuisance that prevents one from leaning back and relaxing.

In turn, men can also feel uncomfortable in complex domestic situations where their actions are limited by rules of avoidance. A fact that is often overlooked by Westerners is that the seclusion of women not only limits the freedom of women but also circumscribes men's behaviour. In the family with whom I lived six months in Sidi Slimane, during the evening that my host was not out to a café to meet his friends he sat in the unheated garage to listen to his transistor radio by the light of a candle. Inside the house the female members of the family were comfortably watching the television in a heated and illuminated room. When a programme was being broadcasted that my hostess thought would interest her husband, she sent out her small daughter to fetch her father. Instead of joining us on the divan, he would sit down on a stool in the far corner of the room and leave again as soon as the programme was over.[8]

Asymmetries in Boundary Control

The discussion of Moroccan notions of privacy illustrates the point that a conception of sex segregation which relegates the activities of women to the 'private' sphere and those of men to the 'public' sphere is too simple. The dominant definition of a situation as private or public as well as the extent to which people are in a position to protect their privacy are dimensions of gender relations. For every social situation the question should be asked vis-à-vis whom amongst the participants is experience of a particular setting felt as private or public. In each case, this implies a process of negotiation between the different participants about their various interpretations of the situation.

The sexual division of Moroccan space is not symmetrical. Men have more space at their disposal than women, and it is easier for men to cross the boundaries of male and female domains than vice versa. The house is considered a female domain, and most men will respect the privacy of the female members of the family by spending much time out of doors. But sooner or later they have to come home to eat and sleep. Also, the house is the seat of the family privacy in which male members of the family participate and which is highly valued by them. Furthermore, as reference to the male head of the household as *mûl ad-dâr*, owner of the house, demonstrates, women are well aware of the fact that house rules are ultimately determined by their husband or the male relative with whom they live.[9]

From this point of view it becomes clear that there is more to the proverb 'A man about the house is like a boil on the back' than was alluded to above. A boil on the back is something beyond your control. You don't have a say in its coming on, and since it is on your back, you can't touch it. In the same vein, a man about the house may be a nuisance that prevents you from leaning back and relaxing, but there is not much you can do about it.

Men never need to ask for permission to enter their house. Women, by contrast, always need the authorization of their husband or male caretaker to go out. To be sure, this does not mean that a woman has to ask for permission every single time she leaves the house. In practice, most women have negotiated a kind of 'passe-partout' or standing permission to visit specific places such as school, the mosque or the public bath, or to leave the house on particular occasions such as to visit a relative or a sick friend. They must, however, always be able to account for their extra-domestic activities, and permission to go out may be withdrawn at any time.

Also, the rules that determine who adjusts to whom when boundaries between male and female spheres are crossed point to asymmetry. The major step a man may take when he enters his home is to call out *camlû at-tarîq* 'clear the way'.[10] Subsequently the women inside adapt to the violation of their privacy by checking their clothing and conversation. Conversely, when women intrude into male domains like the street or the market, they take measures such as veiling, not lingering, or crossing the road to avoid walking past a café. Men make less adjustments to the presence of women in their domains than vice versa. Older and strict Muslim men tend to avert their eyes, while young men not seldom put the trespasser in her place with impertinent glances or remarks.

A form of cultural dominance of men can be observed in these negotiations about the private or public character of places. Women have less control over the boundaries of their private domains than men, and whenever different notions of privacy overlap, women accommodate most prominently. These spatial arrangements correspond to Moroccan notions of male and female corporeality. Men's legitimate penetration of women's private domains reminds one of men's penetration of women's private parts in sexual intercourse. In this way, cultural definitions of femininity and masculinity are embedded in the universals of human sexuality.[11] In the dominant world-view, men are conceived of as bounded entities that are able to exert considerable self-control. This explains why men do not have to take measures when their domains are invaded; it is no threat to their integrity.

Women are considered to have 'open' bodies. Their boundaries are fluid and permeable. Correspondingly, they are thought to have less control over their bodies. Various practices can be observed in which female bodies are symbolically closed. To prevent premarital loss of virginity there are rituals in which girls step through a loom to 'close' their bodies. Also, women must always wear a belt around their waist and keep their hair tied together. Loose clothes or loose hair are associated with loose morals.

Similar relations between the sexual division of space and practices to 'close' the female body as a social measure to control the *Nafs* or passions of women has been documented for other Muslim societies in the Middle East. Delaney (1991: 38) for example, discusses how according to Turkish villagers women must be socially covered under the mantle of a man and enclosed within his home, just as a field must be enclosed and 'covered' by ownership to reap its fruits. This is symbolized by wearing a headscarf. Women who do not wear a headscarf are considered open to the sexual advances of men. Boddy (1989: 53) argues how the cultural definition of femininity in Northern Sudan is closely related to the notion of 'enclosure'. This is expressed in women's confined lives within the enclosure of residential compounds and the practice of infibulation, an extreme form of female circumcision that entails almost complete closing of the vulva. While women explain the significance of this practice in terms of protection of their fertility, men tend to emphasize the need to curb women's strong sexual desires.

These examples appear to agree with the view that sexual divisions in the use of space generally correspond to different conceptions of the moral values of women and men (cf. Sciama 1981: 89). Like Boddy's, my material suggests that because men and women experience space differently they also have differentiated views on male and female moral virtues. My female informants do not acquiesce completely to this dominant view on the 'weakness' of women. In their view the sexual division in the use of space shapes different forms of self-control in men and women. Because of the confined space within which they spend most of their lives, women claim to possess *sabr*, patience or endurance. Unlike men who seek distraction out of doors, women do not run away from their problems but develop the patience to come to terms with them. The salutary effect of *sabr* consists of all that strengthens the religious impulse and weakens the passionate one (cf. Ruska in *Encyclopedia of Islam* 1987: 27). The kind of self-control that men develop more prominently is called *aql*, reason, the adroitness to negotiate successful transactions and act towards strangers according to the Moroccan code of conduct (cf. Eickelman 1989: 181). Contrary to *sabr, aql* is considered to develop as one acquires more autonomy and freedom of movement in the social world.

The Inviolate Privacy of the Public Bath

In the *hammâm*, different notions of privacy and female boundary control concur in a specific combination. Contrary to the house, where women's privacy may be intruded into by male members of the family, the public bath remains a female domain ideally at all times. In terms of gender privacy the public bath is the most private of female domains. The furious response of the bathing women in Halfaouine to the boy whose looks had betrayed him as a man must be understood in the light of the various implications which his trespassing had on female privacy.

With his 'seeing' eyes,[12] the boy violated the only domain over which women have absolute control, the only sphere of privacy that they can legitimately keep to themselves. In a way, the public bath is the ultimate 'circuit breaker' (cf. Moore 1984: 12) for women, a private domain where a social overload, in this case family obligations, can be switched off temporarily. When a woman is out to meet friends, she is expected to come home if her husband sends for her or when she receives word that high status guests have arrived unexpectedly who must be attended to. But in the *hammâm*, a woman cannot be reached from the outside world. Whatever claim people want to put on her must be postponed until her return home. The inaccessibility to outsiders of women in the public bath has even become proverbial; the attention of an absent-minded person with a far-away look is caught by teasingly commenting *mshât al-hammâm*, 'she is off to the public bath'. Not surprisingly, women are ready to defend vehemently the only place where they are temporarily immune to certain demanding obligations.

Losing temper is itself an expression of the relaxation of self-control that is allowed within the female privacy of the public bath. Most *hammâms* are open exclusively to women or to men. Other public baths have separate wings for men and women. Some public baths operate with alternating opening hours or days for men and women. The latter are less popular among women. One woman told me that she is hesitant about visiting a *hammâm* where the men's hours have just finished. She always makes sure that a considerable period of time has elapsed between the departure of the last men and her entrance. She would hate to be the first woman to enter the *hammâm* after it has been vacated by men. She would not feel completely at ease to enter a place almost naked that was occupied by men only shortly before.

My informant's sensitivity to the former presence of men in a public bath illustrates women's sense of bodily vulnerability. For many, the *hammâm* is the only place where, except for their underpants, they undress completely and expose their body and untied hair to others. As Messina describes in her account of the bathing protocol in the public baths in Fez, bathing in the public bath entails much physical contact, bodily intimacy and sensual attention (Messina 1993: 194). This kind of 'openness', of not being constantly on one's guard to protect one's bodily boundaries can exist only because women feel secure that their female privacy will not be violated. Therefore, I suspect that the commotion among the bathing women about the boy's glances also reflects anxiety about having their privacy intruded when most vulnerable.

Also, the presence of a boy who is on the brink of entering the men's world involves the risk of intimate information about women leaking out to male domains. In terms of family privacy, the *hammâm* is the most public of the socially recognized places for women. An additional reason for the turmoil among the bathing women in Halfaouine could well be fear that reputations may be harmed should gossip spread outside the family circle.

Privacy and the Public Bath at the Age of Modernity[13]

In terms of family privacy the public character of the *hammâm* enhances women's vulnerability. Nevertheless this public dimension of the public bath is an important reason for its popularity among women. It is one of the rare places where they meet women who do not belong to their *qurâb* or 'close ones', that is, the circle of friends, relatives and neighbours with whom they interact on a daily basis. Here a woman is likely to pick up news that would not have reached her ears within the close surroundings of her '*dâr wa darb*', the house and the alley where she lives. In the public bath she has the opportunity to extend her personal network beyond the women in her immediate surroundings. The scars and tattoos on the nearly naked bodies of the bathing women tell details of their personal histories without words.[14] This creates an atmosphere of temporary intimacy that may encourage a woman to pour out her heart to any woman who happens to sit next to her. Sharing personal problems with a stranger who has no access to her own social network has the additional advantage that she does not have to be afraid that her confidentialities will leak out to her 'close ones' in the form of gossip that could have repercussions on her reputation. In this way, the weekly visit to the public bath serves as an 'escape' from the family privacy that envelopes women most of the other days in the week (cf. Moore 1984: 46).

Due to modernization processes, the importance of the *hammâm* as a meeting place is not the same for all women. Nowadays, the traditional housing architecture described above is only one of several types that can be found in Moroccan towns. Most high-income families have left the medina or old quarters of the town and moved to the *ville nouvelle*, the former French quarter. The European streetplan and architecture in the *ville nouvelle* look much like high-class suburbs in European cities. Whether they were built during the French occupation or at a more recent date, the lay-out of the modern villas consists of a living room, several bedrooms, a kitchen and a bathroom. The villas are hidden from view by trees and high surrounding walls. Most houses have pitched, inaccessible roofs. Where roofs are accessible, the distance between the houses is usually too large to allow conversation between neighbours. Except for passing cars, the broad asphalted avenues are almost completely deserted. Children do not play in the street but in their private gardens, and corner shops are rare. As a consequence, the hustle and bustle that is characteristic of the traditional quarters in the medina is lacking. Since even the distance between adjacent houses is relatively large and requires passing much open space, women do not easily leave the house for a chat with a neighbour or to run a small errand.

In general the inhabitants of the *villes nouvelles* are financially well-off, and many families have a *khaddâma* or domestic servant. They do the shopping and other chores outside the house, so that the mistress of the house can remain a *hâjba*, a secluded woman. *Hâjbas* only leave the house on special occasions, in which case they put on a face-veil and a *jallâba*, a long traditional overcoat. Even though nearly all houses in the *ville nouvelle* have a bathroom, most women make sure not to skip a weekly visit to the public bath. For many of them, this is one of the rare occasions in their otherwise rather isolated lives when they can meet other women.[15]

The interaction between women in the medina is much more intense. Due to high unemployment and housing shortages, many of the traditional houses as described in the section on Moroccan notions of privacy are now shared by several families, each family occupying a different floor, or, in more dire circumstances, a different room. The central courtyard and the flat roof are shared between the families. To respect the family privacy of the other occupants of the house, men hardly come there, but the women are almost constantly in contact while preparing food on their little mobile charcoal- or gas burners, when doing the laundry near the water tap in the courtyard, or simply relaxing and enjoying the view from the roof in the afternoon. Only small alleys run between the rows of terraced houses so that from their position on the roof women can talk to their next door and opposite neighbours without leaving the house.

The alleys are full of playing children, while hardly a stranger passes by. Not surprisingly, the women in the medinas often leave the house for a chat with a friend who lives a few houses away or to run a little errand at one of the many local shops. When they do not go beyond the immediate surroundings of their house, they do not bother to put on a *jallâba* or overcoat, but casually throw a bedsheet or tablecloth over their shoulders or head. Most of the lower- and lower middle-class families that live in the medina do not have the means to have a domestic servant. Shopping is therefore done by male members of the family or by women themselves. In general then, these women are much more mobile and less isolated than the women in the *villes nouvelles*. For them, a visit to the public bath is a welcome relaxation from the daily household-chores and a good opportunity to talk to women from other neighbourhoods.

As in many modernizing third world countries, the need for cash and commodities has drawn large numbers of people from the countryside to town looking for jobs. The medinas have not been able to absorb the influx of new citizens, and *duwâr jadîd* or 'new villages' spontaneously grow everywhere around Moroccan towns. Like country dwellings, the houses in squatter areas consist of a courtyard with one or two rooms of equal size. Unlike residential patterns in the countryside, the houses are built in rows, forming small alleys that allow the same patterns of interaction between women as was described for the medina. Some of the oldest *duwâr jadîd* now enjoy municipal recognition and are connected to the electricity grid and waterworks. Most squatter areas, however, go without electricity or water. For the daily use of water, women send their children to the public tap to fill empty bottles. Larger quantities of water are needed for doing the laundry, and most women find it more convenient to go to the public tap for this task themselves to do their washing there. To feel more at ease at this public place, they often arrange with neighbours and friends to go there together, so that the public tap has become a meeting place for groups of washing women.

There are no public baths in the squatter areas. The former country people who are living there are not accustomed to visiting the *hammâm* often, since this is typically an urban phenomenon. Nevertheless, adopting the custom of visiting the public bath is an important economic strategy for women from the squatter areas. For these 'newcomers' to town, the economic prospects within the market economy are low and many families depend on extra-market channels of economic and social help. Women from the squatter areas therefore try to gain access to the networks of established women in town and seek to enter into patron-client relations with them.[16] One of the best places to meet townswomen is, of course, the public bath.

What I have tried to argue so far is that besides the attraction of absolute female privacy of the *hammâm*, women from different residential areas and economic backgrounds all have their own reasons for visiting the *hammâm* regularly. Although this may give a fair idea of the importance of the public bath in the lives of women in contemporary Morocco, it is not representative of all Moroccan women. Several categories of women no longer visit the public bath but prefer to bathe at home or visit the public showers.

In the last fifteen years, public showers, sometimes in combination with a *hammâm*, have begun to appear in larger Moroccan towns. In these public showers, people no longer sit in circles on the floor in one of three main rooms behind the buckets of water that they have filled from a communal tap or reservoir. The rooms in the public shower have separate compartments, each with one shower. Each person sits on her own bench in front of her own faucet. This arrangement allows much more individual privacy than the rooms in the public bath. When they first appeared, the public showers were almost exclusively visited by men, but in recent years, more and more women have begun visiting them. I was taken to them by a group of high school girls. They prefer going to the public shower because bathing there is much quicker. You don't have to wait to fill your bucket at the tap, and rinsing the body from the shower is less bothersome than continually having to pour small bowls of water over yourself. Another relatively new category of women composed of secretaries, teachers and other young women with busy jobs, likewise prefers the public shower because of its efficiency.

For quite a different reason, *al-khwatât* or Muslim sisters also show a preference for the public showers over the *hammâm*. Seeking a purer form of Islam, these women disapprove of what in their eyes is the public nudity of bathing women. According to Islamic prescriptions, Muslims should not expose their naked bodies to the eyes of people other than their spouse, and even then, the genitals should ideally remain concealed (cf. Messina 1993: 136). As mentioned earlier, most women in the *hammâm* keep their underpants on while bathing. Some, however, undress completely, covering their genitals with a hand or a washbowl when they traverse the rooms. The Muslim sisters are not the only ones who condemn this behaviour. When I asked women what they liked and disliked about the public bath, exposure to the genitals of other women was often mentioned as one of the drawbacks of bathing there, although few were prepared to avoid the public bath for this reason.

Another disadvantage mentioned by my informants was the lack of hygiene in the public bath. Especially in the public baths in the *ville nouvelle* a growing number of women can be observed who no longer sit directly on the floor. They bring a rubber mat or small wooden stool with them to sit on, thus avoiding contact with the dirty bathing water and the hairs that come off the women behind or next to them. Other women, especially those who have a taken on a European life-style give up visiting the public bath altogether.

To conclude, I would like to take up two points about shifts in the importance of the different notions of Moroccan privacy that I have described in this paper. First of all, it is interesting to note that living in a house that is designed and furnished in a European style which is characterized by a higher degree of space differentiation than traditional houses often goes hand in hand with a growing need for individual privacy and less emphasis on sharing, be it family privacy or gender privacy.[17] Amongst other things, this is expressed in an increasing 'instrumentation' to create more distance between the body and its environment. In the domestic sphere this includes sitting on chairs around a high dinner table rather than sitting on the floor around the *mîda* or small round table; the use of knives and forks and separate plates for the individual members of the family instead of eating by hand from a communal plate; and separate rooms with (single) beds for the children. In bathing practices this involves using devices that prevent direct contact with other bathing women such as rubber mats or wooden stools, or making a shift from visiting the *hammâm* to visiting the public showers where every woman has her own bench and her own faucet.

Secondly, the different categories of women who have stopped visiting the *hammâm* appear to have one thing in common: they tend to have more freedom of movement than the categories of women mentioned earlier. Moreover, this freedom of movement corresponds to several new meeting places for women. Teenage girls meet in school, Muslim sisters meet in the mosque and working women meet at their jobs. The female privacy of these meeting places is not as impenetrable as the public bath. I suspect, however, that the experience of operating outside the traditional female domains implied by their greater freedom of movement has developed a stronger sense of individualism in these women which may have diminished the importance of gender privacy for them.

Notes

1. I first explored the significance of the *hammâm* to women during research in 1983-4 in the town of Sidi Slimane, Morocco. This resulted in a (Dutch) master's thesis in 1986 in which I discuss the importance of the public bath for women in 1) creating and sustaining social networks, 2) participating in the community of Muslims by adhering to Islamic notions of purity and purification, and 3) marking transitions that women make from one stage of life to another through specific bathing rituals. In 1992 and 1993 the first public baths for Moroccan and Turkish women in the Netherlands were opened. In the meantime, I had developed a specific interest in the relation between the gendered experience of religion and the construction of (Moroccan) female identity as a result of my Ph.D. research into the meanings of fasting for women during Ramadan (Buitelaar 1993). These circumstances led me to take a fresh look at my earlier material and extend it with new fieldwork in the Dutch *hammâms*. This paper is mainly based on the 1983-4 material.
2. Cf. Nelson 1974, and Rogers 1975.

3. Ardener, 'Ground rules and social maps for women: an introduction', in Ardener 1981.
4. Much to the annoyance of high school students, who have difficulty finding a quiet place to do their homework. Many of them take their books to the parks or sit down under a street lantern. This behaviour is more readily accepted from boys than from girls, who face the additional difficulty of being expected to participate in household chores.
5. I use this emic term since it allows more room for personal links between non-kin that may have developed over time as a result of common residence, fosterage, ongoing relationships after dissolved marriages and so on. Cf. Eickelman 1981: 156-62.
6. 'Even after gaining access to the initial opening, one is not yet within the main part of the household, but rather one must first follow a dark, circuitous hallway that finally breaks forth in the central courtyard - a place of great pleasure. The image is clear. Entry into the female is difficult, but if one gains access, then pleasures abound' (E. Combs-Schilling 1989: 215).
7. Cf. Moore 1984: 46, who maintains that escape into such a group is never a complete escape from social demands. While offering temporal escape from external pressures, intimate groups also serve to transmit and sustain different aspects of a society's culture. Therefore such groups develop their own standards of behaviour. That is one of the reasons for continuing individual ambivalence toward such groups, a tendency to retreat into an intimate protective group and then to escape from it.
8. Cf. P. Bourdieu, 'The Kabyle house or the world reversed' (1979: 141), who describes for Kabyle society in Algeria how men are 'shut out' of the house in daytime; also H. Geertz, in the essay 'The Meanings of Family Ties' in C. Geertz, H. Geertz, L. Rosen (1979: 331) we are presented with descriptions of how men in Sefrou, Morocco, move with circumspection in their own neighbourhoods and homes.
9. The *Mudawanna* or Moroccan code of personal status follows Malikite law according to which it is a man's duty to provide maintenance for his wife, including a place to live. In return

for her maintenance, the wife owes the husband her faithfulness and obedience. Cf. L. Buskens, *Islamitisch Recht en Familiebetrekkingen in Marokko. Aspecten van wet en werkelijkheid in de steden Rabat en Salé en het omliggende platteland*, Amsterdam: Bulaaq (forthcoming).

10. F. Mernissi cited in Messina 1993: 117.

11. Compare Combs-Schilling 1989: 215 who writes about the mingling of such undeniable givens and cultural assumptions: 'The fusion of the two ... makes it difficult for the female to distance herself from the cultural definitions because they are written on and through her own body. To discard the definitions would be in some real way to damage her essential self ... The embedding of cultural particulars in universal thoughts is one of the most powerful and durable means of reproduction that culture has available to it.' On this last subject, also see Connerton 1989.

12. The mistress of the public bath allows women to bring along their sons until they begin *teyshûfû* or *tey^{c}arfû* 'to see' or 'to know', meaning that they begin to view the naked female bodies with a sexual interest.

13. For the purpose of this paper I use Bernal's definition of the term modernity: the process of incorporation into the nation-state and the capitalist world economy. Cf. Bernal 1994: 36-67.

14. Tattooing is a form of traditional therapy to treat various illnesses such as infertility and spirit possession. Cf. Akhmisse 1985: 87-8.

15. Cf. Messina who cites the Moroccan proverb according to which: 'A woman only leaves the house to go to the *hammâm* and the cemetery' (Messina 1993: 187).

16. For analyses of such informal female networks for other categories of North African women see: Maher 1974 and Jansen 1987.

17. I owe this argument partly to Messina's description of domestic spatial arrangements in the Moroccan city of Fez, although she does not make a clear distinction between family privacy and gender privacy (Messina 1993: 114,194).

References

Akhmisse, M. (1985), *Médecine, Magie et Sorcellerie au Moroc,* Casablanca: Benimed.

Ardener, S. (ed.) (1981), *Women and Space. Ground Rules and Social Maps,* London: Croom Helm.

Bernal, V. (1994), 'Gender, Culture and Capitalism: Women and the Remaking of Islamic "Tradition" in a Sudanese Village', *Comparative Studies in Society and History,* vol. 36, no. 1.

Boddy, J. (1989), *Wombs and Alien Spirits,* Madison, Wis.: University of Wisconsin Press.

Bourdieu, P. (1979), *Algeria 1960,* Cambridge: Cambridge University Press.

Buitelaar, M. (1993), *Fasting and Feasting in Morocco. Women's Participation during Ramadan,* Oxford/Providence: Berg Publishers.

Cammaert, M. (1985), *Migranten en thuisblijvers. De leefwerld van Marokkaanse Berberwrouwen,* Assen: van Gorcum.

Connerton, P. (1989), *How Societies Remember,* Cambridge: Cambridge University Press.

Combs-Schilling, E. (1989), *Sacred Performances. Islam, Sexuality and Sacrifice,* New York: Columbia University Press.

Delaney, C. (1991), *The Seed and the Soil. Gender and Cosmology in Turkish Village Society,* Berkeley: University of California Press; New York: Columbia University Press.

Eickelman, D. (1989), *The Middle East. An Anthropological Approach,* Englewood and Cliffs, N.J.: Prentice-Hall.

Elias, N. (1969), *Über den Prozess der Zivilisation. Soziogenetische und psychogenetische Untersuchungen* (2 vols), Frankfurt am Main: Suhrkamp Taschenbuch Verlag.

Encyclopedia of Islam (1987) vol. VII, Oxford: Oxford University Press.

Geertz, C., H. Geertz and L. Rosen (1979), *Meaning and Order in Moroccan Society. Three Essays in Cultural Analysis.* Cambridge: Cambridge University Press.

Jansen, W. (1987), *Women without Men. Gender and Marginality in an Algerian Town,* Leiden: Brill.

Maher, V. (1974), *Women and Property in Morocco. Their Changing Relation to the Process of Social Stratification in the Middle Atlas,* Cambridge: Cambridge University Press.

Messina, M. (1993), *Celebrations of the Body. Female Spirituality and Corporeality in Muslim Morocco,* Ann Arbor: UMI Dissertation Services.

Moore, B. (1984), *Privacy. Studies in Social and Cultural History,* Armonk, N.Y.: Sharpe,Inc.

Nelson, C. (1974), 'Public and Private Politics: Women in the Middle Eastern World', *American Ethnologist,* vol. 1, no. 3.

Rogers, S. (1975), 'Female Forms of Power and the Myth of Male Dominance: A Model of Female/male Interaction in Peasant Society', *American Ethnologist,* 2.

Rosaldo, M. & L. Lamphere (1974), *Women, Culture and Society,* Stanford: Stanford University Press.

Sciama, L. (1981), 'The Problem of Privacy in Mediterranean Anthropology' in S. Ardener (ed.), *Women and Space: Ground Rules and Social Maps*, London: Croom Helm.

Chapter 5

Female Dervishes in Contemporary Istanbul: Between Tradition and Modernity

Catharina Raudvere

Even in popular media, it is more and more recognized that groups and individuals associated with religious activities in the Muslim world cannot always be identified as part of 'the Islamist movement'. All Muslim activities are certainly not 'Islamist', on the contrary many Muslims react strongly against Islam's new visibility in society. Among religious organizations in Turkey, the various Sufi orders play an important role. In what is a complex debate the participants take up very different positions and formulate very different strategies. Some of the Sufis strongly oppose what they consider to be authoritarian attempts of manipulation. Therefore it is important to identify religious opposition against what is casually known as 'Islamism'. As Michael Meeker writes: 'The resurgence of Islam in Turkey is better understood as a transformation, rather than a revival, of religiosity' (1995: 31).

This article is based on preliminary fieldwork among urban women in Istanbul, with a special emphasis on strategies used by women attached to Sufi groups towards the Islamic presence in contemporary Turkish society.[1] As we shall see, young educated women have changed many formerly indisputable facts about secularism, religion and modernity. In the official republican discourse religious observance used to be associated with rural and small town people with little or no education. Today there is a multitude of religious strategies for women and numerous more or less formal organizations providing different outlooks on attitudes, ritual practices, dress and so forth.

Sufism is a very broad term, covering a wide range of different Muslim groups and activities, as well as theological and philosophical assumptions, over a long period of time.[2] It can generally be defined as the mystical traditions of Islam. A dervish is an initiated member of a Sufi order, emphasizes personal spiritual development and the obligation to follow the instructions of their teacher, a sheik, who is also the spiritual leader of most prayers and ceremonies. Sufi groups, far from homogeneous, are found in all parts of the Muslim world and among immigrants in Europe and North America. Mostly these dervish orders are organized in formal, semi-public communities, but the ritual practices of Sufism have also always been observed in private throughout history. Sufism has a long and complicated history beginning in the very first centuries of Islam (Baldick 1989: 13). The early Muslim mystics were to a great extent influenced by Christian ascetics in their mode of contemplation and devotion. The repetitive prayers developed into the principal ceremony of all Sufi groups, and found legitimation in the Koran (Chittic 1987). Via Eastern Christianity influences also came from Indian spirituality, such as meditation, breath control and the use of the rosary (Baldick 1989: 23). Most Western scholarly works concentrate on Sufism as a theological system or as literary history, and only few address ritual practices among Sufi groups.[3] The emphasis on doxa, normative and philosophical systems, and not least aesthetics, have formed an exceedingly idealized image of Sufism as an attractive form of expression. Sufi conceptions have been transformed into Christian terminology in search of transhistorical similarities and eternal truths. Poetry and the world of art have in many ways formed the image of Sufism as a more beautiful and acceptable form of Islam than the general idea of Muslim orthodoxy. Through the metaphors of wine drinking poets and beautiful women the image of the lustful Orient has been maintained. Sufism has been used by European artists and writers as a form of self definition, presenting themselves as outsiders, in opposition to narrow-minded bourgeois respectability, but not necessarily as Muslims.

The affluence of roses and nightingales in the Orientalist studies of Sufism has created a great distance between the normative and 'life as lived'.

Sufi Women in History

It is hard to trace women of flesh and blood in Sufi history, though some female saints appear in pious legends (Baldick 1989: 29). Most frequently Rabi'a of Syria appears, and is often treated as a single historic person. But according to Julian Baldick's convincing analysis it seems more likely that stories about two women, Rabi'a of Basra and Rabi'a of Syria, have been amalgamated into one character in legendary history. Rabi'a is commonly referred to in the religious education of young women, not only in Sufi contexts, as an ideal to follow. Her life is told in pamphlets and popular booklets and she is especially renowned for her 'absolute devotion to the love of Allah', as I was told. The life of the saint can, it seems, easily be related to women's lives in the mega city of today. Some scholars have emphasized the way in which Sufi philosophers of the Middle Ages use female imagery when constructing metaphors of the Divine, above all Ibn 'Arabi (d.1240). From 'the golden age' of Persian and Turkish poetry a highly idealized imagery of women appears in poetry and pious literature; an image of the ideal female, rather than descriptions of women's lives.[4] The 'positive role' of women in Sufi literature as stressed by Anne-Marie Schimmel is mainly an interpretation of literary sources, not analysis of lives of historical women. 'As mothers, many mystically inclined women have deeply influenced their sons who in turn became leading masters of the Path thanks to their early education' (Schimmel 1982: 145). The contrast is very sharp between Anne-Marie Schimmel's literary study and Julian Baldick's historical approach. Her appendix 'The Feminine Element in Sufism' in *Mystical Dimensions of Islam* (1975) refers only to idealized women in poetry or legendary history. Similarity and stability are stressed rather than difference and change, while Baldick does not hesitate to show how both theology and religious practice were reciprocally influenced.

It is undeniable that side by side with the exquisite poetry praising women of both beauty and spiritual qualifications many negative theological conceptions are associated with women. The influence on Sufism from the gnostic aversion of the human body and the physical aspects of life led to many very negative statements about women in general. The use in Sufi theology of negative philosophical terms, in different ways associated with femininity or women, emphasize this dichotomy (Schimmel 1975: 112; Watson 1994: 144). Traditional Sufi training, the 'path', aims at controlling human nature and man's given conditions: body and soul. It is a striving upwards away from what is considered material and therefore associated with the feminine. It has been pointed out many times that the soul on its lowest level was considered feminine, grammatically as well as philosophically.

Only brief notions in historical documents tell of female members who participate in prayers and other activities of the dervish orders.

Turkish Islam and Secularism

Turkey differs in several ways from many other Muslim countries and the conflicts between various religious and more secular groups have a long history (cf. Toprak 1981, 1987, 1994; Mardin 1983, 1989, 1994; Baykan 1990; Kafdar 1992; Zürcher 1993; Markoff 1994; Sayarn 1994). 'Islam in Turkey always was, and continues to be multi-dimensional' Richard Tapper (1991: 3) writes in his introduction to *Islam in Modern Turkey*. Along with urbanization and other changes within the social structures, modernist educational programmes from the 1920s onwards led to the situation in Turkey today where secularism, traditionalism, nationalism, and Islamism intermingle in ideological struggles at all levels of society. The Turkish political arena cannot be sufficiently described in right-left categories, since it involves harsh conflicts of social, ethnic and religious character.

Governmental religious politics of the last 70 years have been dominated by a programmatic secularism attempting to transform Turkey into a 'modern' European society. The reform ideology has its origins in the nineteenth-century Ottoman *Tanzimat* movement and other attempts to introduce Western reforms, but at the time secularism to a large extent was met with reluctance (Ahmed 1993, Zürcher 1993). At the beginning of this century the so-called Young Turks, took up these attempts at modernization in their struggle against the old Ottoman rulers. Ever since Mustafa Kemal Atatürk gained power in 1923 after the fall of the Ottoman empire, systematic secularism has been on the agenda. His government initiated what is commonly known as 'the republican revolution': a series of radical changes (*devrimler*) 'revolutions' or 'turns'. Among the first measures taken were restrictions on the religious communities. All Muslim activities came under state control and became to a large extent mosque-centred, as pointed out by Richard and Nancy Tapper (1987b), while other places for religious devotion were shut down.

A chain of changes involving radical transformations of Turkish society started with the abolition of the caliphate in 1924. The dervish orders were forbidden by legal restriction in 1925, although they have remained active underground ever since. The meeting places of the Sufi orders, (the *tekkis*) were closed, along with them the institutes of religious education (*medreses*), and welfare institutions of different kinds. All of them were dependent on the *vakifs*, foundations closely linked to the religious establishment and forbidden at the same time. Other places for gathering, like holy shrines of saints and great sheiks (*türbes*), popular destinations for pilgrimages, were also closed. The use of religious titles such as *sheik, efendi, baba* and so on, and garments and other attributes associated with the Sufi orders were prohibited. The consequence was, as Richard Tapper writes, that 'Turkish Islam in effect became more standardized, circumscribed and compartmentalized' (Tapper 1991: 2).

This large modernization project run by the new leaders, with grand political ambitions, led to significant changes — many of them with an immediate effect on everyday life. As signs of modernization, the alphabet was altered from Arabic to Latin script, the Gregorian calendar was introduced, and the use of family names. The symbolic value as well as the practical 'not only gave Turkey a more European image, but also made communication with the Western world much easier' as noted by Eric Zürcher (1993: 231).

The tempo and intensity of the reforms were met with some reluctance and led to opposition and even violent uprisings (Yalman 1969). After Atatürk's death in 1938, and even more so after the elections in 1950, when Adnan Menderes formed the government, the pressure on religious groups was reduced (Zürcher 1993: 231). During this period 'religious courses were brought back into education, government support of the *Hac* (the annual pilgrimage) was restored, shrines were reopened and training for religious officials was restarted' (Tapper 1991: 9). But still, it must be remembered that education on all levels as well as all aspects of the official discourse was based on secularism and nationalism. Religion was not an obvious topic on the political agenda until the late seventies.

Secularism and Nationalism

Turkish secularism was markedly nationalistic from the beginning. Ziya Gökalp (d. 1924), the ideologist of Kemalist secularism, *layiklik*, formulated a patriotic national ideology in which the search for the pure, original, Turkish heritage was an important part. *Öztürk*, original and true Turkish, was one of the key terms (Olson & Öztopçu 1993: 2). The ancient Turkic nomads of Central Asia and the Anatolian peasants were highly idealized, despite the latter being the most devoted protectors of Muslim traditions. In the Kemalist ideology, modernity was identified with what was Western and European. Words like *oryantal* and *arabesk* were used, and still are, with strong pejorative associations, meaning both Eastern (Arabic) and an inclination to be backward and anti-modern. What are thought of as ideals from pre-Islamic periods, democracy and equality between the sexes, were linked to the new ideals of modernism. Linguistic purism also belongs to this era, hailing Turkish as the mother of all tongues, with the result that popular culture was even more influenced by Arabic media: radio stations, films and so on (Stokes 1992: 89).

As early as the Ottoman period, a nationally defined religion was prevalent, a distinct Turkish form of Islam, in which Sufi theology played an important part. Sufism is defined by the dervishes themselves as liberal and individual. These two aspects are united in a generally cherished assumption that genuinely Turkish traditions are maintained among the Sufi orders. Among the contemporary orders, often in opposition against secular politics as well as Sunni orthodoxy, other alternatives for a pious life are at hand than those offered by the Islamic groups. The attitudes towards Sufi orders are somewhat ambiguous. Despite legal restrictions and counteractions against them, they are highly regarded by people in general as preserves of genuinely Turkish traditions. Legends, stories of miracles, poetry, songs and instrumental music are known to be transmitted among the dervishes, particularly the poems of Yunus Emre (d. ca. 1321) (Schimmel 1975: 329). The consequences are a rather complicated situation where the dervishes are both oppressed and honoured. The Islamist universalism, therefore, stands in many religious and political questions in glaring contrast to Turkish nationalism. In individual lives, however, this is not always a conflict.

Secularism and Women in Turkey

The history of the women's movement in Turkey goes back to the nineteenth century and involves both religious and secular groups (cf. Ahmed 1982, 1984; Kandiyoti 1991). The Turkish mode of secularism also has a very special relation to women's issues. Education of women was one of the foremost targets of the Kemalist campaigns and served as an icon of modernity. Modern educated women were called 'the daughters of the revolution', a phrase still used on and off in conversation. Rapid changes were promoted by the Kemalist government and the secularization process was encouraged, from the early nineteenth century onwards. This created a divergence between different levels of education and tensions between rural and urban lifestyles in republican Turkey, 'a society that had been exposed to an élite-directed radical transformation of traditional values regarding women', as Feride Alcar (1991: 281) writes. The rural-urban tension has remained a basic theme in much writing on life in contemporary Turkey. However, in the last twenty years rural life has moved into the big cities, as much as the image of the 'city' and the modern world is presented through TV and other media in the countryside. Sharp divisions are no longer made so easily.

The Halveti-Cerrahi Order of Istanbul

A Sufi order is called a *tarikat*, that is a path or road, hinting at the spiritual development offered members of the group. The principal ritual, the repetitive, intense *zikir*[5] prayer ('remembrance') is observed by almost all dervish orders. The term is used several times in the Koran (10: 71, 21: 48, 21: 105 and 40: 54) a fact which has served as an important defence for the Sufis against orthodox criticism of Sufi piety as affected and sentimental.

Among the Sufi orders in Turkey, the Halveti-Cerrahi has a unique position. It is the only one officially recognized, and goes by the name of a 'society for traditional Turkish music and folklore' *(Türk tasavvuf musikisi ve folklorunu araşturma ve yasatma vakfi)* (Kissling 1953; Jong 1965; Martin 1972; Baldick 1989: 114). The community is a branch of the Khalwatiyye and has a long history as an urban Sufi order in Istanbul (cf. Jong 1965; Baldick 1989). The dervishes meet three times a week at the *tekke*, the lodge of the *tarika*, a place of devotion and social gathering. The *tekke* consists of several houses and looks rather small and insignificant from the street. At the entrance is the mausoleum, the *türbe*, with the founder's coffin and his imitators' coffins covered with green cloth. These holy men are shown tokens of veneration by the dervishes when entering or leaving the *tekke*. Pir Nurredin al-Cerrahi (d. 1721) founded the *tekke* in Karagümrük, where the dervishes still meet, in 1704. Today, this is quite a run-down part of Istanbul, near Fatih, a district known among other citizens to be a centre for Islamists. To religious people it has a certain flavour of tradition and Muslim history.

Many of the orders' activities are focused on the founders, venerated at their mausolea. Genealogies and succession form a vital part of the oral history of the orders. Everyday events discussed among the dervishes are often referred to in connection with a legend from the life of the founder or one of the important sheiks and how God guides him through trouble and difficulties to harmony and order.

Both male and female dervishes are disciples *(mürids)* of the sheik, and are supposed to follow the ideal of training and developing themselves. Hierarchies among the dervishes form the basic infrastructure, with the sheik at the top. He is responsible for the dervishes' spiritual development, being the teacher of the community, and the leader of rituals, and through interpretation of dreams he gives individual guidance. Secrets are supposed to be revealed on the steps toward perfection. From the point of view of the dervishes, the hierarchies symbolize spiritual development and are shown by signs on their garments. The hierarchies of the past and the present exist in a way simultaneously: important persons of the past are present through story-telling and the teachings of the sheik and gives authority to his statements and decisions.

In the 1960s and 1970s the Halveti-Cerrahi order led a languishing life and only a few men kept up the *zikir* prayers in Karagümrük. For the past fifteen years there has been a steadily increasing interest due to the charismatic sheik Muzafer Ozak (d. 1985) and the new Islamic appearance in Turkish society. These factors have rendered two new groups of members: Western converts, often familiar with meditation and new-age rituals, and many of them women; and also young Turkish people without family ties who enter the order. Ozak had a developed programme for his mission. Many of his books are translated into English and he went 'on tour' to the USA and Europe to preach his message and perform public *zikir* ceremonies on stage with a group of dervishes. They represent the new *şeriat*[6] orientation, closer to a stricter interpretation of Muslim ideals, while others are fascinated by the musical and poetic heritage among the Halveti-Cerrahis, an attraction that can be described in religious as well as nationalistic terms.

Rituals among the Halveti-Cerrahi Women

Evidently, there have been women of greater or less importance throughout Sufi history, but hardly anything is known of how they practised their religion. How regular was their attendance at the *tekke*? How frequent were their *zikir*-meetings at home? How were the hierarchies constructed among women compared to men? Many of these historical questions seem hard to answer, despite the fact that the history of the order plays such a great role in the narrative traditions of the group. Today's female Halveti-Cerrahi dervishes cannot be said to conduct parallel activities; rather, I find the image of a Chinese doll more relevant. The male dervishes act on the fringe of a public arena, while the women's activities and rituals are even more hidden. Not on purpose, as far as I can see, but they are just considered less important and less suited for public encounters.

From my observations I can distinguish three groups among the female Halveti-Cerrahi dervishes. The first is the elderly women who frequent the *tekke* as part of their family traditions. Many of them were born in the countryside. The middle-aged women constitute the second and the smallest group. Like the elderly, their acquaintance with Sufism springs from the family, and they are socially well integrated in the order. The third group, that of young women, is very heterogenous. It consists partly of not very well-educated women, often at home with small children. Like the older women they generally come with other family members, and the better part of their social network is within the order. A new kind of member has joined the order over the past few years — well-educated young women, many of them professionals or university students. Membership is to them a personal choice, and they are fully aware of what the head-scarf and the long skirt symbolize in secular society. These often very well-spoken young women represent the new visibility of Islam, the movements and tendencies in Turkish society today. Their aspirations and aims — how they construct 'tradition' differently for different purposes — indicate the complexity of the conflicts that the Halveti-Cerrahi order confronts today. It is no longer a question of secular versus religious matters; the religious is certainly polyphonic. In many families it is a source of conflict between the generations.

This is so not only in the construction of meaning within the traditional frameworks of history and story-telling: a new şeriat-orientation is also present. This new generation of well-educated women has a positive outlook on religion, and plays an active part in society to a much greater extent than previous generations. With their different lives they will have new expectations and demands on the order in the future.

Every Thursday *zikir* is performed by the dervishes. For some hours before the ceremony, about 75 women of all ages come slowly dropping in at the women's part of the *tekke*, and many more during Ramadan, the month of fasting, and other festivals. Some come very early for social reasons and sit and chat before the prayers start. They can reach the women's part of the *tekke* directly by way of a staircase on the outside of the main building without moving through the men's part at all. The upper floor has several rooms for social activities and meals, and doors to the gallery above the *büyük meydan*, the prayer room of the male dervishes. The Thursday meetings follow a set pattern: first evening prayer, then dinner with night prayer to follow, that turns into *vird* (a litany composed by Pir Cerrahi), and then finally the *zikir*-prayer which can last for several hours. During this intense ceremony some of the '99 beautiful names of God' are repeated for long intervals. As the tempo, the bodily movements and intensity of the *zikir* increases, the male dervishes rise and form a spiral, while moving in circles.

In the crescent-shaped gallery the women sit very close to each other in the crowded room, and it is almost impossible to move. It is very hot and dark. The women follow the *zikir* in the same way as the men do. But they cannot rise, or form any circles. Although I pointed out several times that I had no intention to convert, my interest in the group was interpreted as an indication that I 'had a good heart'. I was always welcome to attend the *zikir* prayers. With a scarf on my head I sat in the back row of the women, but mostly I was urged to sit in the front row with a good view over the *büyük meydan*. It is questionable, however, to what extent the separation between the sexes should dominate an analysis when it is not emphasized by the participants themselves. The spatial distance between men and women is so conspicuous to a Westerner that it tends to become the fundamental category for descriptions and interpretations. When asked, women mostly answer that they perform *zikir* together with the men, but at different locations of the *tekke*. After a while distinct groups of women were recognizable to me. They had their set parts of the gallery and any trespass resulted in quarrels. Space was also marked by age (elder women in one corner), attitude to dress (from peasant style to sumptuous *hijab*) and different emotional intentions in the participation of the *zikir* ceremony.

Not all women taking part in the *zikir* are initiated members, *dervişler*. From the neighbourhood women come more or less regularly to the various meetings at the *tekke*. It can be women with a general interest, but women on a pilgrimage to Pir Cerrahi's tomb are also rather frequent visitors. The latter are often members of some of the many Halveti sub-groups and come on organized bus tours.

Women's *Zikir*-ceremonies

Once a month the women come together for a *zikir*-ceremony of their own. On these occasions no man is present at the *tekke*, and all duties are performed by women. It has been difficult for me to find out whether these gatherings are a recent phenomenon or not. Different persons give very different answers. A plausible assumption seems to be that the various kinds of meetings that Turkish women traditionally have held in their homes are now made into a public ritual, open to anyone who chooses to come. Domestic gatherings of a more or less religious character have been important arenas for women's religious practices.

These movements from domestic to more public arenas is most likely an impact of modernization processes in everyday life. In the suburbia of the modern metropolis it is no more possible to hold meetings restricted to family and friends. Other places than the traditional arenas open up for women's gatherings. The choice of where to go and which leader to follow plays a crucial part in the construction of an urban Muslim identity.

The women's *zikir* at the Halveti-Cerrahi is led by two women appointed by the sheik. A fact of utmost importance for the women going across Istanbul on their own is that the meetings can be attended guarding their modesty. A room adjoining the gallery (not circular like the *büyük meydan*) is used for these meetings. However, this room is so overcrowded that the women cannot rise and, to my knowledge, they invariably perform *zikir* sitting down, even under more private conditions. Despite this, the intensity is as ardent as on Thursdays. The prayer is accompanied by heavy bodily movements and fervent emotional expressions. The *zikir* starts gradually, reaches its climax and fades slowly away while the women sing *ilahiler*. Pieces of sugar and candy that have been placed close to the *zikir*-leaders during the ceremony are afterwards distributed among the participants. Bottles of water and garments from the sick are also collected after having received *baraka* from the *zikir*. Tea, snacks and sweets are shared in small groups, while some women remain with the *zikir*-leaders and talk to them, maybe sharing some confidence. Others continue to sing *ilahiler* and yet others enter the rooms next to the prayer-room for a chat and other social activities.

The social importance of the order for the members cannot be overestimated, bearing in mind the considerable increase of the population of Istanbul over the last 50 years and the almost uncontrolled growth of the major cities. In contemporary Istanbul most women of the Halveti-Cerrahi order are newcomers in a metropolis of more than 12 million people facing inflation, unemployment, housing shortage, and overcrowded flats. Many families are split because of work migration. The women experience a strong social identity with the group in Karagümrük, where they can form new bonds and relations. As Fulya Atacan (1990) has shown, the order offers male networks of economic contacts as well as being a basis for other important relations, both personal and professional. To a certain extent this is also true for women's religious activism. Affiliation to a specific group gives access to new arenas.

Headscarves and the 'New Veiling'

'Why are women's heads the site of political and religious conflict?' Carol Delaney asks in an article on the social and political meanings of bodily hair (Delaney 1994: 168). And certainly *tesettür*, the proper covering of the body, has been a constant topic in the Turkish debate just as in most other Muslim countries.

The Kemalist laws of the 1920s never mentioned female dress but regulated only the men's headgear. Still, the female headscarf (*başörtü*) has been regarded as either rural and backward or ostentatiously religious. Its reappearance in the public arena was to some elder secularists both a threat and an insult to the Kemalist ideals. Since the early 1980s, young women started to come to university campuses with covered heads, although the law prohibited religious clothing in official areas. These Islamist women put on new designs and outfits, claiming them to be 'traditional'. None of these garments were used in pre-republican Turkey. Rather it is an invented tradition, globally used by women as a sign of Islamic consciousness. In Turkey Atatürk himself has for decades served as a model for secularist outfit: clean shaven, with a business suit and tie, sometimes a bowler hat, his portraits hanging on the wall of almost every official building and in many private homes (Meeker 1995: 37). His wife and daughters played the same role as public persons with their short European dresses and short uncovered hair. In the first decades of the republic the different modes of clothing were interpreted as indicating a struggle between urban and rural, between educated sophistication and ignorance. The Koran, the primary source of Muslim ideals, states that a true believer, man or woman, should be dressed in a modest way. What modesty *(edep)* implies has caused an intense debate (Olson 1985; Mandel 1989; Zürcher 1993: 302; Delaney 1994; Ilyasoglu 1994; Watson 1994) and different Muslim groups have different answers as to what constitutes proper clothing.

'The veil' has for a long time served as a popular Western icon of the position of Muslim women. But it has also been emphasized that 'headscarves' and 'veils' can be interpreted as a revolt. 'Debates about the new veiling force all women to recognize that choice of dress is both a personal and political matter. It may be one of the few forms of political protest some women have' Watson (1994: 157) writes in a highly discerning article on the interplay between norms on female dressing and local practices. This is certainly true as long as this insight does not create other 'absolute images' of Muslim women in the media. It must be remembered that many Muslim women do not accept the Islamist specification of 'veiling' or implementation of *şeriat* as the only relevant mode of guidance for their wardrobe or religious practice. In their interpretation of religion, more covering of the body is not the equivalent of a higher grade of religiosity.

A rich variety of Muslim dress can be observed in the streets of Istanbul, from the all-covering black cloaks *(çarsaf)* to what are considered to be country-style scarves, *başörtü*. The Arabic term *hijab* is sometimes used by radical Islamists referring to proper Muslim clothes for women. The different modes of the *tesettür* is a fashion in its own right. Shops specializing in modest clothing offer their customers variations of monochrome full-length coats and matching headscarves in discreet patterns. Also, the all-white headscarf can be decorated in a number of ways: woven patterns, beads, fringes or lace. Although spoken of as a 'uniform' by many secularists, the marks of individuality are unmistakable. The variations can easily be 'read' in the street or on campus as identification of adherence to particular groups and attitudes. In the academic world opinions are evidently divided as to whether the *tesettür* is a question of personal choice or an expression of a repressive ideology. The importance of outward signs and appearance is certainly not restricted to women. The way men handle their facial hair is equally interpretable. Being shaved and wearing a tie, like Atatürk did, is a clear sign of secular ideals, while the moustache is generally regarded as the 'traditional Turkish look'. A more strict and sober appearance with a well-cut beard and a long-sleeved white shirt without a tie, but buttoned up, is rather common among men within various Islamist groups. The male dress has not created the same conflict nor hindered young men's entry to university or professional life; whereas many well-educated women wearing *tesettür* feel discriminated and trapped between two sides on the labour market knowing most employers' negative attitude towards the wearing of headscarves. When I asked a young unemployed civil engineer whether she had tried religious manufacturers, she answered bitterly: they only hire men.

External appearance and clothing are very much in focus, not only in the general debate, but also among religious women themselves. Helen Watson stresses how varied the attitudes operating towards the appearance and movement of the body can be within a Muslim community. 'Less attention has been given to the personal and political dimensions of *hijab* as both a required form of dress and a personally chosen article of clothing' (1994: 143).

Constructing Urban Muslim Identities

The women who perform *zikir* at the Halveti-Cerrahi *tekke* differ as much among themselves as religious women in general do in contemporary Istanbul. The image of Turkish Muslim women has been deconstructed over the last years by second wave feminist and religious women alike and no single prototype can represent the complexity of approaches. These processes have also encouraged women's religious activities and they have moved more into the public arenas from the private realm. 'The woman question' is regularly discussed in the media and the way the Islamists deal with the issue challenges the secular establishment and is highly provocative to many loyal Kemalists. The members of the Sufi orders certainly do not stand unaffected by the intense debate in the media.

Religious Turkish women relate in very different ways to the debate on Islam's influence on public matters. To some it is a question of degree, while others, like some female dervishes, consider the Islamist claims to be fundamentally contradictory to their Sufi ideology. The demands for an Islamic influence on society are part of intricate global processes, but in Turkey they are also flavoured with a programmatic secularism and the imperial history of the country. Due to the Turkish educational system, secularism is the one background everybody can relate to, whichever position is taken in the debate on the relationship between the state and religious activities.

It seems likely that Turkish women, in the past as well as the present, form informal religious groups to a larger extent than do men, with meetings at home, votive prayers and vows at shrines and cemeteries. At Koca Mustafa Pasa Camii, where the saint Sümbül Efendi and his daughter Rahine are buried, a huge tree grows. This has been for long a place of special importance to women. The type of piety expressed here is of the kind Islamists as well as secularists condemn. Private prayer meetings are frequently and severely criticized by Islamists as a breeding ground for superstitious behaviour and un-Islamic tendencies in general. In Islamist rhetoric women's gatherings beyond the control of local imams and mosque oriented hierarchies are often associated with uncontrolled Sufi activities. From a secular point of view the Sufi orders have the means of establishing invisible networks and thereby have a certain political influence. The presence of these orders also blurs attempts at a clearcut categorization of contemporary Muslims.

Women of the Halveti-Cerrahi order are part of a formal organization with longstanding rules of internal structure and rituals. The oral history of the community has always functioned as a way of interpreting the experiences and choices of the dervishes. Many women also take part in informal gatherings that seem to vary more than the restricted ritual life within the Sufi order.

Being a young female dervish in contemporary Istanbul is to claim both tradition and modernity. The normative discourses founded in the Koran and in the *hadith* offer transhistorical claims which are used to defend a variety of positions. However, in a rapidly changing social context — a steadily growing metropolis with social turbulence and political turmoil — interpretation of the holy texts is an absolute necessity to be able to construct an urban Muslim identity. The collapse of Kemalist modernism is highly visible in the postmodern city with its dissolved centre, its problems of uncontrolled settlements and pollution. In the midst of this are women's lives. Nevertheless, being a religious woman is not any longer equivalent to ignorance and powerlessness. It can certainly also mean resistance to authoritarian Islam.

Notes

1. The fieldwork was conducted in the autumn of 1993 and summer of 1994, altogether four months. Generous grants from Bergvalls Stiftelse and Erik Philip Soerensens fund made these visits to Istanbul possible.
2. General surveys with further references include Schimmel 1975, Awn 1987 and Baldick 1989.
3. Some studies that emphasize rituals of specific Sufi groups are Trimingham 1971; Gilsenan 1973 and Geels 1993.
4. Emilie Olson and Kurtulus Öztopoçu write in their discussion on how to evaluate and use the poetic sources as indications of Sufi women's lives (1993: 11): 'the use of feminine imagery as a metaphor for God in poetry of both Turkish and non-Turkish (Arabic and Persian) mystics may also suggest, on the one hand, that in contrast to more orthodox Muslims, Muslim mystics tended to have a more positive if sometimes idealised view of women in profane as well as sacred realms. On the other hand, the mystical poets who do not refer to either males or female specifically may also reflect the general lack of differentiation which is characteristic of Sufi thought, leading them to use androgynous or non-sexual models of human beings in relation to that which is sacred.
5. Referred to and usually transliterated as *Dhikr* in Arabic.
6. Islamic Law usually transcribed as *Sharia* from Arabic.

References

Alcar, F. (1991), 'Women in the Ideology of Islamic Revivalism in Turkey', in R. Tapper (ed.), *Islam in Modern Turkey*, London: I.B. Tauris.

Ahmed, F. (1993), *The Making of Modern Turkey,* London: Routledge.

Ahmed, L. (1982), 'Feminism and Feminist Movements in the Middle East, a Preliminary Exploration: Turkey, Egypt, and People's Democratic Republic of Yemen', *Women's Studies International Forum,* vol. 5, 153-68.

Ahmed, L. (1984), 'Early Feminist Movements in the Middle East: Turkey and Egypt', in Frieda Hussain (ed.), *Muslim Women,* London: Croom Helm.

Ahmed, L. (1989), 'Arab Culture and Writing Women's Bodies', *Feminist Issues,* vol. 9, 41-51.

Arat, Y. (1990), 'Islamic Fundamentalism and Women in Turkey' *The Muslim World,* vol. 80, 17-23.

Atacan, F. (1990), *Sosyal degisme ve tarikat Cerrahiler,* Istanbul: Hil Yainlari.

Awn, (1987), 'Sufism', in M. Eliade (ed.), *Encyclopedia of Religion,* vol. 15, 104-23, New York: Macmillan.

Baldick, J. (1989), *Mystical Islam,* London: I.B. Tauris.

Baykan, A. (1990), 'Politics, Women and Postmodernity', in B.S. Turner (ed.), *Theories of Modernity and Postmodernity,* London: Sage Publications.

Chittic, W.C. (1987), 'Dhikr' *Encyclopedia of Religion,* vol. 4, 341-44, New York: Macmillan.

Delaney, C. (1991), *The Seed and the Soil: Gender and Cosmology in a Turkish Village,* Berkeley: University of California Press.

Delaney, C. (1994), 'Untangling the Meanings of Hair in Turkish Society', *Anthropological Quarterly,* vol. 67, 159-72.

Gardet, L. (1965), 'Dhikr', in *Encyclopedia of Islam* (2nd ed.), vol. 2, 223-7, Leiden: Brill.

Geels, A. (1993), 'A Note on the Psychology of Dhikr', in T. Ahlbäck (ed.), *The Problem of Ritual,* 53-82, Stockholm: Almqvist & Wiksell.

Gilsenan, M. (1973), *Saint and Sufi in Modern Egypt,* Oxford: Clarendon Press.

Ilyasoglu, A. (1994), *Örtülü kimlik,* Istanbul: Metis Yayinlari.

Jong, F. (1965), 'Khalwatiyya', *Encyclopedia of Islam* (2nd ed.), vol. 4, 991-3, Leiden: Brill.

Kafadar, C. (1992), 'New Visibility of Sufism in Turkish Studies and Cultural Life', in R. Lifchez (ed.), *The Dervish Lodge: Architecture, Art, and Sufism in Ottoman Turkey*, Berkeley: University of California Press.

Kandiyoti, D. (1991), 'End of Empire: Islam, Nationalism and Women in Turkey', in D. Kandiyoti (ed.), *Women, Islam and the State*, London: Macmillan.

Kissling, H.J. (1953), 'Aus der Geschichte des Chalvetijje-Ordens', in *Zeitschrift der Deutschen morgenländischen Gesellschaft*, vol. 103, 233-89.

Mandel, R. (1989), 'Turkish Headscarves and the Foreigner Problem', *The New German Critique*, vol. 46, 27-46.

Mardin, S. (1983), 'Religion and Politics in Modern Turkey', in J.P. Piscatori (ed.), *Islam in the Political Process*, Cambridge: Cambridge University Press.

Mardin, S. (1989), *Religion and Social Change in Modern Turkey*, (SUNY series in Near Eastern studies), Albany: State University of New York Press.

Mardin, S. (1994a), 'Culture Change and the Intellectual', in S. Mardin (ed.), *Cultural Transitions in the Middle East* (Social, Economic, and Political Studies of the Middle East 68), 189-213, Leiden: Brill.

Mardin, S. (1994b), 'Islam in Mass Society: Harmony versus Polarization', in M. Heper & A. Evin (eds), *Politics in the Third Republic*, Boulder: Westview Press.

Markoff, I. (1994), 'Popular Culture, State Ideology, and National Identity in Turkey', in S. Mardin (ed.), *Cultural Transitions in the Middle East* (Social, Economic, and Political Studies of the Middle East: 68), 225-35, Leiden: Brill.

Martin, B.G. (1972), 'A Short History of the Khalvatiyya Order of Dervishes', in N. Keddie (ed.), *Scholars, Saints and Sufis*, 275-305, Berkeley: California University Press.

Meeker, M. (1995), 'Oral Culture, Media Culture, and the Islamic Resurgence in Turkey', in E.P. Archetti (ed.), *Exploring the Written*, Oslo: Scandinavian University Press.

Nasr, S.H. (1987), *Traditional Islam in the Modern World*, London: KPI.

Olson, E. (1985), 'Muslim Identity and Secularism in Contemporary Turkey: The Headscarf Dispute', *Anthropological Quarterly*, vol. 58, 161-71.

Olson, E. & K. Öztopçu (1993), 'Images of Women in the Poetry of early Turkish Mystics and the Status of Women in Turkish Society', in H.W. Lowry and D. Quataert (eds), *Humanist and Scholar: Essays in Honor of Andreas Tietze*, Istanbul and Washington: ISIS Press.

Sayarn, S. (1994), 'Islam and International Relations in Turkey', in S. Mardin (ed.), *Cultural Transitions in the Middle East* (Social, Economic, and Political Studies of the Middle East: 68), Leiden: Brill.

Schimmel, A. (1975), *Mystical Dimensions of Islam*, Chapel Hill: University of North Carolina Press.

Schimmel, A. (1982), 'Women in Mystical Islam', *Women's Studies International Forum*, vol. 5, 145-51.

Stokes, M. (1992), *The Arabesk Debate*, Oxford: Oxford University Press.

Tapper, N. (1983), 'Gender and Religion in a Turkish Town', in P. Holden (ed.), *Women's Religious Experience*, London: Croom Helm.

Tapper, N.(1985), 'Changing Wedding Rituals in a Turkish Town', *Journal of Turkish Studies*, vol. 9, 305-13.

Tapper, N. & R. Tapper (1987a), 'The Birth of the Prophet: Ritual and Gender in Turkish Islam', *Man* (N.S.), vol. 22, 69-92.

Tapper N. & R. Tapper (1987b), 'Thank God we're Secular!': Aspects of in a Turkish Town', in L. Caplan (ed.), *Studies in Religious Fundamentalism*, London: Macmillan.

Tapper, N. & R. Tapper (1990), 'Ziyaret: Gender, Movement and Exchange in a Turkish Community', in D.F. Eickelman & J. Piscatori (eds), *Muslim Travellers*, 236-255, London: Routledge.

Tapper N. & R. Tapper (1991), 'Religion, Education and Continuity in a Provincial Town', in R. Tapper (ed.), *Islam in Modern Turkey*, London: I.B. Tauris.

Tapper, R. (ed.), (1991), *Islam in Modern Turkey*, London: I.B. Tauris.

Toprak, B. (1981), *Islam and Political Development*, Leiden: Brill.

Toprak, B. (1987), 'Islamist Intellectuals of the 1980s in Turkey', *Current Turkish Thought*, vol. 62.

Toprak, B. (1994), 'Women and Fundamentalism: the Case of Turkey', in V.M. Moghadam (ed.), *Identity, Politics and Women*, Oxford: Westview Press.

Trimingham, J.S. (1971), *The Sufi Orders in Islam*, Oxford: Oxford University Press.

Watson, H. (1994), 'Women and the Veil: Personal Responses to Global Process', in A.S. Ahmed and H. Donnan (eds), *Islam, Globalization and Postmodernity*, London: Routledge.

Yalman, N. (1969), 'Islamic Reform and the Mystic Tradition in Eastern Turkey', *Archives Européennes de Sociologie* vol. 10, 41-60.

Zubaida, S. (1995), 'Ernest Gellner's Sociology of Islam', *Economy and Society*, vol. 24, 151-88.

Zürcher, E. (1993), *Turkey a Modern History*, London: I.B. Tauris.

Chapter 6

Women and Muridism in Senegal: The Case of the Mam Diarra Bousso Daira in Mbacké[1]

Eva Evers Rosander

Introduction

In Senegal one finds various forms of the current, 'traditional', 'local' African Islam, comprising mainly Sufi Islam. There is also another orientation of Islam which is less 'traditional' and more 'global', an Islam more open to the universalistic Islamist tendencies and expressions of today. I refer to Islamization as a kind of mediator between tradition and modernity in Senegal, being at the same time an interface and a dividing line between local and global and between traditional and reformistic or radical. In this article, my main focus will be women and Sufi Islam in Senegal. More precisely, I am interested in Murid women, the Muridiyya being the second largest *tariqa* ('path', religious Sufi 'order' or 'brotherhood') in Senegal, and the Murid women's associations. I have particularly studied one religious association, dedicated to the veneration of the mother of the founder of Muridism, the famous Sheikh Amadou Bamba. This association carries the name of the mother, Mam Diarra Bousso. The image of the mother as a pious person whose influence on her son results in his turning into a great saint is very important in Sufism in general and perhaps even more so in its West African form. The mother figure is central in West Africa also outside the realm of Sufism. The woman as a mother has an undeniable status and even a certain authority which is not the case for women without children.

My interest in women's organizations in West Africa derives
from a conference a few years ago with a group of Scandinavian
and West African female social scientists. We called it
'Transformation of Female Identities: Women's Organizational
Forms in West Africa'. The working title of my research project
is 'Women's organizations as cultural expressions of female
identity'. It has been carried out in Mbacké, a town situated 180
km. east of Dakar, close to the Murids' holy city of Touba.
Mbacké was the town where Sheikh Amadou Bamba spent part
of his life before he moved to Touba, which has since then
become the centre of Muridism. In my field work I have been
concentrating on the women members of the Mam Diarra Bousso
association. Through participation in their meetings and visits to
their homes I have tried to get an idea of their lives and ambitions
and of their engagement in the association. Together we made the
pilgrimage to Porokhane to celebrate the memory of Mam Diarra
Bousso in January 1995. In January 1996 I was back in Mbacké,
ready for the annual *magal* (pilgrimage) to Porokhane, but this
year it was postponed until March due to a cholera epidemic.

The main purpose of this article is to show Senegalese female
religious practice in the Muridism of today. I will first briefly
present the Murid brotherhood and then give an account of the
Murid gender ideals as manifested in the legends about Mam
Diarra Bousso and in the Murids' daily life. Murid institutions
such as the *dara* (rural working 'camp' and Koranic school run by
a marabout, i.e. a religious leader) and the *daira* (religious
association) will be introduced, and the Mam Diarra Bousso
association will be described in some detail. In the final analysis
of the Mam Diarra Bousso members' religious practice it is not
only seen as linked to the dominant religious ideas and concepts
but also interpreted in terms of women's ability to 'manipulate'
the value system without challenging it nor aiming at changing it.

Women's Informal Associations

In my article I will, as mentioned, mainly concentrate on women's
participation in one particular, more or less informal, religious
association. I call this form of association 'informal' as it has no
links whatsoever with the state or with state related regional
institutions. Even if there exists an elected president and a cashier,

one or several secretaries and someone who makes the accounting for the money which is collected from the members, there are no membership lists or any forms of registration. To cease being a member does not require any formalities; one just stops going to the meetings.

Generally speaking, women's informal associations in Senegal not only provide a collective basis for action - they also express and consolidate women's cultural identities. In the Senegalese society everybody strives to become integrated into the group. Nobody wants or can stay alone, without belonging to one or more groups. To be alone is to be 'outside', isolated, and that is something which only mad people do. Ones life has to be 'transparent' (Wolof: *leer*) and well known to the social surrounding. This is ones social and moral obligation as a woman and a good and socially acknowledged member of the community. Everything has to be done in common as if to underline ones honesty: meals, work, entertainment. The associations offer the proper framework and the legitimate form for togetherness. *Aide-entre aid* (self help) is important for all kinds of social activities and ceremonies. This means collaboration with others on a reciprocal basis. To realize oneself fully as an individual, one needs a group, a collective.

Religious and ritual associations draw upon a higher authority. To better explain what I mean I will cite Kathryn March in her article about women's associations and development: 'The religious associations cast women's actions within a culturally meaningful frame, cloaking women's associations with an aura of spirituality, inspired authority and orienting the place of gender in the wider world order' (1982: 78). This will be my perspective in the following in my use of the Mam Diarra Bousso association as a case for analysis of women's position in the local community as well as for making some tentative generalizations about their place in the wider society. In a similar way, I will discuss some religious institutions and rituals from the point of view of gender ideology and practice. To clarify these issues they will be divided into questions about religious *authority* and the relations between those who have and those who have not access to religious power. The nature of *leadership* and member *participation* in the religious associations are also matters of concern. The participation of the members is often motivated by both self-assertiveness and self-protection as part of women's informal strategies. The focus easily enough becomes directed towards the distribution of material and immaterial resources. The associations are informally structured around female communication networks which also stretch into male domains of power and authority. Another focus is the moral reputation of the women leaders and members of the associations, reputations which sometimes can be more or less successfully manipulated by the women. This leads us to reflect on female and male ideas about Murid gender ideals. Mam Diarra Bousso is, as we shall see, one such female religious ideal person, whose life is told again and again in the form of legends by the Murids as an example of the ideal wife and mother whose behaviour was characterized by patience and the ability to keep family secrets and endure hardships.

Some Analytical Concepts

For my analysis there are three key words or concepts, namely *purity, religious education* and *religious blessing*, which are intimately linked to men's and women's different positions in the religious institutions and rituals. Those key concepts in the male dominated Islamic discourse are often brought up in Senegal by the Sufi marabouts as well as by the Islamists. They can be said to be *paroles d'honneur* of the Senegalese Islamic revival. And they affect women's participation in Muridism, as Sufism and Islamism are partly interacting and influencing each other in contemporary Senegalese society.

Perhaps 'birth' is the factor of most importance for the position of women in Senegalese society. 'Caste',[2] religion, ethnicity, descent from the great maraboutic lineages - all this gives ascribed status to women, as well as to men, of course. However, compared to women, there seems to be more transactional space for men's social careers; men are socially more mobile and their careers more unconventional. The male status seems to be more easily achieved and transformed in other, alternative and overlapping ways, like for example in connection with migration. Women's role as moral icons of the society prevents them from getting recognition for certain more innovative forms of status changes. In relation to blessing, descent is decisive for both men

and women, as we shall see. But again, women have the disadvantage of obtaining much less societal recognition for the
blessing they have inherited from their maraboutic lineage through
descent, although they may be *sokhnas*, i.e. of maraboutic descent
or married to marabouts. In short, women give and receive less
blessing than men. This contributes to their marginalization in
public life in relation to the men, whose ideas about themselves
and the women dominate and monopolize the gender ideology and
its religious as well as its secular practice.

By purity (Arabic: *tahara*) is meant ritual purity, required of
those who approach God through prayers, reading of the Koran,
entering holy spaces like the mosques, and so on. These people
are men, as women who menstruate and give birth are impure
during their bleeding periods. The blood is considered defiling.
This physical fact predestines women to a second-rate position
within the Muslim gender hierarchy, as a woman cannot control
her blood shed and thus cannot avoid being periodically 'unclean'.
It limits her participation in the rituals and contributes to giving
her this low ranking compared with men.

Religious education and knowledge has always been an
important criteria for being a Muslim. Knowing Arabic well
enough to be able to read the Hadith and knowing prayers and at
least parts of the Koran by heart are current examples of what is
defining true believers of Islam. *Jahaliyya,* religious ignorance, is
now becoming a negatively loaded moral concept, signifying not
only as it did originally the lack of Islamic knowledge which
characterized non-Muslims living outside the Islamized regions.
Added to this, today the concept has connotations of heresy or
even denigration of Muslim values. Religious education for both
girls and boys is today on the Islamists' agenda all over the
Muslim world. This is not necessarily so, however, among the
Sufi leaders. It is true that knowledge of Arabic, being the
religious language, is prestigious and increasingly winning ground
also among the Sufis. But the Murids still consider their religious
identity as closely linked to Wolof (ethnic) identity and to the use
of the Wolof language. Poor families, and particularly girls and
women of poor families, remain illiterate and ignorant, something
which contributes to their subordinated position in relation to men
in religion.

Religious blessing (Wolof: *barke*, Arabic: *baraka*) is a comparatively unique male quality, linked to male descent of the maraboutic lineages. Concerning the religious blessing, women from maraboutic families do inherit *baraka*, like men, but to a lesser extent, and they have access to it and get recognition for it on negotiable and highly varying conditions. Personality is probably more important then descent for the recognition of female *baraka*. The transfer of blessing through men is a phenomenon whose importance cannot be stressed enough, when criteria for religious authority, for example, are discussed in a Sufi context. The marabout's crucial role in a *tariqa* is intimately connected with his ability to give *baraka* to his disciples. In relation to this, the importance of religious merit (Wolof: *tiyaba*) for women should not be neglected. The work they do and the money they offer to their marabouts give them religious merit, which is perceived as something being directly rewarded them by God. Men as well as women get *tiyaba* for their pious acts, of course, but women seem to be more in search of it than men, as their possibilities to get *baraka* through the mediation of the marabouts are more limited (Buitelaar 1994).

The Murid Brotherhood

The Muridiyya is an Islamic brotherhood of great political, economic and social significance in Senegal. Even if the brotherhood is not the biggest one in terms of number of disciples, it has many characteristics which are usually considered as typical of the Senegalese form of Islam and Islamic mysticism or Sufism. The biggest brotherhood in Senegal is the Tijaniyya; another important one is the Quadiriyya.

The Murids are effectively organized in a country-wide federation with its administrative and religious centre in Touba. The most eminent group of the leaders belong to the same lineage as the founder or are allied to him through marital alliances. The fact that the leadership is well organized gives the dominating Murid leaders a power position in Senegal, which the other brotherhoods partly lack. This power derives to a great extent from the Murids' active participation in the economic life of the country and their indirect links to the Senegalese state. The religious ideology encourages economic activities. Resources from the marabouts' disciples in the form of agricultural work on maraboutic properties - above all the peanut cultivations - or cash from the urban religious associations pour in to the great religious leaders. The political power is considerable, as the Murid leader in Touba can mobilize masses of people through proclaiming an order (Wolof: *ndigeul*) to his disciples to vote in favour of the candidate preferred by him.

In the Murid brotherhood the religious leader who followed after Sheikh Amadou Bamba (1850-1927), is called *khalifa general*. He is recruited patrilineally. The present *khalifa general* is one of the two remaining sons of the founder. When they die, the grandsons of the founder will be eligible. Other direct descendants of the founder (often indicated by being called Mbacké, i.e. related to Sheikh Amadou Bamba both matri-and patrilineally) also become sheikhs or *sokhnas* (there is just one daughter still alive) and have the right to their own disciples, called *talibés*. They are about ten in number and constitute *les grands marabouts*. Ranked as of lower status in the Murid hierarchy are the *petits marabouts*, who are greater in number and more remotely related to the Mbacké family (Magassouba 1985: 31). The base of the hierarchical pyramid consists of the Murid disciples, whose obligations are to show deference and obedience to the sheikh or the *khalifa* to whom they are attached. The Murid brotherhood distinguishes itself by a total subjection of the disciple towards his leader. This is expressed through the disciple giving a promise of obedience, to the sheikh, or, as he is often called in the francophone literature, the marabout. The link between *talibé* and sheikh is basic for the existence and functioning of the brotherhood. It cuts through family ties and ethnic and regional belonging. Furthermore, it is considered to be a masculine relation: women cannot maintain such a link with a religious leader except under very special conditions (see below), as women are not allowed to pronounce the vow of obedience (Wolof: *djebelu)* to the sheikh. The sheikh's *baraka* (Wolof: *barke*) will strengthen and help the disciple in his life on earth. Through the mediation of the marabout and his holiness, the disciple hopes to gain access to an eternal life in paradise. The link to the marabout also works as a kind of social security net for the disciple, who will, for example, be able to count on the sheikh's support for marrying his children and paying the costs in relation to that.

The founder, Sheikh Amadou Bamba, stressed the importance of the male disciple's unconditional work duty for his marabout, whenever the latter demanded it from his *talibé*. The Murid emphasis on work as a religious duty has not been given any thorough theological explanation by the founder. It remains clear, however, that the stress on work refers to work for ones marabout; it does not refer to being industrious as a general virtue. Agricultural work could already in Sheikh Amadou Bamba's time replace religious education for the rural disciple. In this respect Muridism differs from the Tijani brotherhood, which pays greater attention to religious formation and to education. Muridism was and is associated with the rural areas of Senegal and with the Wolof ethnic group, although there are many exceptions to this. The Murid language is Wolof; French is not considered proper to use.

The Ideal Wife and Mother: Mam Diarra Bousso

The Senegalese gender relations seem to be both conflicting and contradictory, partly interacting, partly clashing with each other in everyday life. Two discourses distinguish themselves particularly among several others concerning male-female relations in Senegal. The Islamic discourse emphasizes women as subdued and patient beings, while the 'African' discourse stresses motherhood, the mother having a strong, powerful as well as a loving and caring personality. As a mother, she is of greatest significance for the well-being of the children. Particularly as a Wolof mother, she is considered to predestine her children to success or failure in life through her own moral behaviour (see below). Following the Sufi tradition the pious mother is seen as the ideal fosterer of the Sufi saint. Thus, she is considered to have a great influence on her children's spiritual development.

The mother image of Mam Diarra Bousso, the mother of Sheikh Amadou Bamba, fulfils both the Wolof and the Sufi ideal expectations. She is frequently referred to in Murid women's conversations as an example for all women to follow. Through the numerous legends about her life and behaviour, which are transferred orally from one generation to the next, she occupies a central place in the Murid moral universe. Her popularity is immense, not least because of her strong mystical potential. The women say that Mam Diarra Bousso gives to them what they ask for within a year. She assists the afflicted people who come to her tomb (Wolof: *khabru)* in Porokhane asking for her help more rapidly than even her much more famous son, Sheikh Amadou Bamba. His tomb in Touba is visited by over a million people each July on the biggest of all the Murid *magal*s. According to the legends, Mam Diarra Bousso's characteristics as a wife coincide with those of the ideal Murid and Wolof woman. She is patient (Wolof: *muñ*), she endures without complaints whatever hardships and injustices her husband may expose her to and she finds proper means of providing for her husband and children in hidden ways, not blaming him or making him embarrassed for not being able to support his family. The main concept is *soutura*, to have or to show *soutura*. The word has Arab origin, indicating a veil or a piece of cloth which is used to hide things, like a kind of wall. In this case it is mostly the misdeeds or bad luck of the husband which should be hidden. The wife is expected to conceal unpleasant secrets about her family life and to appear stoically and bravely as a happy wife without problems. Public negative information about the husband has to be avoided so that he does not appear to be a mean person in the judgement of others (Ly: 252-64).

These ideal female characteristics are vividly illustrated in the legends, which are known among most Murid women, constituting a female oral tradition. One of them tells about Mam Diarra Bousso's unselfish way of financing the family's food costs, when her husband was not able to give his expected share. The good-hearted woman went without complaints or reproaches with her necklace to one of the Fulani (Wolof: *peul)* who lived outside the village each day to buy milk and millet for the husband, the co-wives and all the children, paying each day with a pearl. When Mam Diarra's mother came to visit her, the old woman asked for the necklace. Not until then did the daughter tell her mother what she had used it for. The mother was impressed by the good behaviour of Mam Diarra and bought all the pearls back from the *peul* as a gift to her daughter. This is a really pedagogic example of *soutura*, shame, and willingness to conceal the truth, protecting the husband from the blame of others for his inability to provide for his family.

Another popular legend shows the extraordinary *muñ,* patience, of Mam Diarra and the total submission she showed to her husband. One evening the husband wanted to go outside the homestead to do his ablutions and Mam Diarra accompanied him to open the gate. On his way back he never told her to close the gate and join him to sleep. Instead he forgot about her and went to rest, while Mam Diarra spent all the night at the gate, the rain pouring down on her, waiting for her husband to call for her. Not until early the following morning did he miss her, called for her and asked her where she had been. When telling him the truth he was astonished over her patience, her obedience and her strength to endure hardships.

As a mother, her qualities are also expressed in terms of honesty and transparency. The general idea is, that the fate of the child is strictly dependent on his/her mother's moral behaviour. This places a heavy burden on the mother, who will alone be made responsible for her children's actions; their success as well as their failures in life. On the other hand, the father's good or bad influence on his children depending on his own manners as a family member is reduced to none. Here descent is not mentioned in relation to female behaviour, but morality, and women's social responsibilities, which seem to be much greater than men's. Motherhood really means something, as stressed above, and Mam Diarra Bousso has to be given thanks and glory for getting a son like Sheikh Amadou Bamba. It is only thanks to her own stainless moral life, her patience and ability to persevere and endure personal sufferings that Muridism has such an extraordinary founder and religious leader as Sheikh Amadou Bamba. This is eloquently expressed in one of the legends in the following way: The little baby learnt miraculously early to talk. He was just a few years old when he told his mother in confidence that he was a saint, a prophet, and that it was because of her that he had this power. It was due to her submission and obedience to her parents, and most of all to her husband, the child's father, that she had got a son like him. 'You are worth it and I will never be anybody else's but yours and only yours', said the baby boy who was to become the great Sheikh Amadou Bamba to Mam Diarra Bousso.

Male and Female Murids

The ideal male Murid dedicates his physical strength, time and labour to serve his spiritual leader without complaint. To submit, to obey orders, to be good, peaceful and hospitable are all male Murid virtues. Women seem to be almost invisible in such religious structures as brotherhoods of the kind here described. They have no other task than to provide food to the men working in the maraboutic fields or to prepare food for the religious feasts. As they are not supposed to make the vow of obedience and subjection to the sheikh, they cannot be considered to be proper Murid *talibés*. Besides, the women should have the same relation to their husbands as the husbands have with their marabouts; i.e. a relation characterized by submission and obedience. This is how women have been pictured in some of the literature on Muridism, probably reflecting the opinions of the social and political scientists' Senegalese male informants (O'Brien 1971; Copans 1980; Creevey 1992). This is certainly not the female Murids' view.

When women are asked about how they perceive themselves as Murids, they state that they are the followers of a certain Murid sheikh because of their membership in a certain *daira,* religious association, which venerates him or the *khalifa general* in Touba. They say they often have the same sheikh as their husband and if not, they have the same as their fathers. Membership in the religious associations makes them feel as active participants in the brotherhood.

It is true that the women cannot become *imams,* religious teachers at the mosque, just as they cannot, according to prevailing norms, be religious leaders, have disciples, give vows of obedience to their marabout and sing the *qasaid*, the religious songs written by Sheikh Amadou Bamba, containing citations from the Koran. However, exceptions from these 'prohibitions' can easily be found in Senegalese religious practice. To avoid misunderstandings, we have to distinguish between 'ordinary' female Murid *daira* members and wives and daughters of eminent religious leaders, the latter being called *sokhnas*. What is possible for these women, who belong to famous and powerful maraboutic families, is impossible for the great majority of Murid women. The ideological reasons presented by the Murid men fall back on the Islamic gender ideas about women as being ritually impure - and moreover ignorant, lacking religious education.

One cited example of a *sokhna* (daughter of a famous sheikh) with exceptional power and influence is *Sokhna* Magot Diop, who inherited her *barke* from her father *Serigne* (a title awarded the great male marabouts) Abdoulaye Niakhep. Already as a child she was chosen by her father, who did not have any surviving sons, to become his successor because of her charismatic personality. She lives in close contact with the *khalifa general* in Touba. Even if she is a woman she has given him her vow of obedience. Her father decided that this should be done and nobody opposed. *Sokhna* Magot Diop has considerable political power in the Thies region, where she lives, because of her disciples' loyalty and her many influential connections. Thus, this female marabout has her own male and female *talibés* (Coulon 1988; Coulon and Reveyrand 1990).

It is also true that the 'ordinary' Murid women from non-maraboutic families offer their religious leaders their ability to make food and in connection with this their time, labour, and, not least, their money. They also provide sexual services and reproductive capacity in the maraboutic polygynous marriages. Young girls are given as brides to the sheikhs by their *talibé* fathers. These marriages often take place without legal marriage contracts, which means without any possibility to get a legal divorce. Not until a marabout 'frees' his wife by telling her that she can leave is the marriage cancelled.

The Dara

The Murid *dara* is connected with the rural areas and its Murid population. The word itself has Arabic origin (*dar*: house) and was before the rise of Muridism the name of the place for religious education, primarily Koranic studies. In the first phase of Muridism the *dara* was an effective instrument of the Murid sheikhs' colonization of the rural areas of Kaolack, Thies and Diourbel. The disciples of the great marabouts cleared the land and cultivated great quantities of peanuts on the maraboutic fields.

Today the most frequent form of *dara* combines agricultural work and religious education for the sons of the Murid farmers, who live in villages 'owned' or controlled by the sheikhs. There is certainly social pressure on the farmers to send their sons to the *daras*, as well as to contribute their own labour in the maraboutic 'Wednesday field' once a week, as a matter of fact often on a Wednesday. Many of the Murid farmers came to the maraboutic villages as landless peasants, receiving their fields from the hands of their sheikhs. Others got their land from the marabout or his father after having spent some years themselves in the *dara*.

There exists a female equivalence to the *dara* for the daughters of the disciples' families. The wives/wife (the *sokhna*) of the marabout receive/s small girls who are left from the age of four to five by their mothers in the maraboutic household to live with the *sokhna*, to work for her and to be educated by her as a sign of their loyalty to and confidence in her. The daughters are given the name of the *sokhna* by their parents, who have wanted to honour her, according to the current tradition. In these female maraboutic collectives the girls grow up in big groups, without close contact with their mother. She just comes and visits the *sokhna* on certain occasions, such as the religious feasts and after childbirth. The mother stoically avoids showing too much tenderness towards her daughter on these rare occasions, so as not to make the departure from the *sokhna* difficult or painful. The girls stay with the marabout's wife until they become married. It is the *sokhna* who chooses a husband for the girl and helps with the wedding costs as well as the organization of it.

The Daira

Dairas are mostly associated with urban forms of Muridism. Currently, however, not only *daras* and 'Wednesday field' work but also *dairas* are found in the Murid countryside. The popularity of the *dairas* grew in parallel with urban migration, which started to assume considerable proportions in the 1950s. They originated in the immigrating Murids' need for an instrument in town by which people could regroup themselves according to the criteria prevalent in the city without losing their identity as Murids, even if they were living far from their marabout. The *dairas,* which, as mentioned above, constitute religious associations devoted to a certain marabout or to the *khalifa general* himself, have an important task in the urban political as well as religious life. *Dairas* offer a visible and concrete measure of the influence and fame of a particular sheikh - he is needed by his disciples because of his *baraka*, but he certainly also needs his *talibés* to manifest, confirm and maintain his power position in relation to other sheikhs - and he needs the financial contribution from the *daira* members (Diop 1981).

Members of the *dairas* are mostly sons, daughters and grandchildren of urban migrants. The organizations are divided according to age and to a certain extent according to sex - men and women sit separately although in the same room. In these *dairas*, in which both women and men are members, men tend to control the important posts, while women have a structure for formal representation parallel to and beside the men's. Thus, there is a women's president and a men's president of the same *daira*. Women certainly have a great deal to say in the *daira*'s operations, even if Senegalese society, including the *dairas*, is characterized by its stratified social structure and its resulting hierarchical norms.[3]

Some *dairas* are based on the members having a common profession, others on vicinity, others have members who suffer from the same handicap - for example being blind. Other *daira* members have nothing in common except the marabout. Different ethnic groups, 'cast' and 'non-cast' people and immigrants from different regions of Senegal, may be found among the members in one and the same *daira* in Dakar or in any other city. In the rural village all the *daira* members come from the same section of the village, 'belonging to' the same marabout, who usually lives nearby.

At the weekly meetings, religious songs are sung, issues related to the activities of the *daira* are discussed and the weekly sums of money are collected. These sums — the so-called *addiyya* — are given to the *daira*'s sheikh and/or to the *khalifa general*. The two leading persons, the president and the treasurer, are elected or should ideally be elected by the members. They are very important and influential individuals and often the only representatives of the *daira* who have any direct contact with the marabout. The great exception constitutes the yearly pilgrimage to the marabout and/or to Touba (Wolof: *magal*), to see the *khalifa general*. Then all the members join together for the pilgrimage. The membership in a religious association is more or less voluntary, although the disciples' participation may be a forced one, due to social pressure from the neighbourhood. According to information from some social workers in the town of Mbacké this is sometimes actually the case, especially for poor and divorced women, who have to be especially careful about their moral reputation. However, membership in a prestigious marabout's *daira* means forming part of a social network, which could provide poor women with access to otherwise hidden resources.

Female Participation

Even if the *daira* is not at all a particularly female phenomenon, it fits very well into other forms of women's organizations, be they *tontines* (Wolof: *nat*), saving associations, or *mbotaye*, social self help associations. Not only in the Muridiyya but also in other brotherhoods, the presence of women in the *dairas* is remarkably strong and their participation often intense. Women contribute considerably both with money and work to the practical arrangement of the *daira* activities and with the preparation of food to all the religious feasts. They help actively in the organization of the *gammous*, which in the Muridiyya context means religious meetings with especially invited guests who sing religious songs and give speeches on religious subjects. However, due to the fact that they are women, and considered impure or polluting because of their menstruation periods (see above), they cannot perform the most important initiation ritual, the vow of obedience, to their sheikh. Neither do they take an active part in the singing of the religious songs. Of course they are allowed to sit listening to the men's singing, which is what they do for hours. However, there are some songs, not containing Koranic citations, which they can and do sing. I am now referring to fertile women; women in other phases of life are not considered impure and therefore the restrictions on them are less severe.

The *dairas* are formed by the board and the disciples/members, not by the marabouts themselves — they take no initiatives and most of them remain in their rural villages, far from the urban

activities of the *daira*. Just once a year they receive their disciples
and *daira* members who make a pilgrimage to their marabout to
leave him the money they have collected during the year. He uses
it ideally for giving food and shelter to the poor, to the visitors
during the *magal,* pilgrimage, and for ameliorations of the
community in which he lives (construction of mosques and so on).
Sadaqa, alms, are given to the *khalifa general* in Touba on the
yearly pilgrimage in July, the greatest Murid manifestation of the
year, when the Murids assemble in Touba to celebrate the
memory of their founder, Sheikh Amadou Bamba.

The Mam Diarra Bousso *Daira*

The Mam Diarra Bousso *daira* in Mbacké was presented to me as
a women's *daira*. This made me confused, as I had never heard
about anything similar. Being in a preparatory stage of my fieldwork (Spring 1992) when I did not trust my own ability to
understand what actually went on around me, I asked to have an
interview with the president, who was a woman. This was not so
puzzling, after all, for, as already described, the women members
of the mixed *daira*s have their own president, to which the female
members address themselves in practical matters. The president,
however, reassured me that this was a female association whose
members celebrated the memory of Sheikh Amadou Bamba's
mother, Mam Diarra Bousso, through their common activities.
These consisted in collecting money for the annual pilgrimage to
Porokhane in southern Senegal and to go together there each
January.

My surprise was great to find a female *daira* in such a male-
dominated society. This was even more puzzling considering the
fact that most women were illiterate, and said to be unable to
manage money of any great quantity. *Daira* members acting
outside the very intimate and informal context of the household
and the *mbotaye*, 'self-help´ groups, where contributions were
interchanged between the women for rites-de-passage party
purposes in cash, cloth or soap was something new. Here other
demands were raised. Going on a pilgrimage to Porokhane
required organizational skills as it was a long journey, comprising
two days absence from home, which meant hiring a vehicle and
bringing food. There was also a moral component: women should

not be travelling around without men, 'for fun'. My assistant laughed at my worries and said that this was a feminist *daira*. These were strong and capable women. But on my question why they had chosen the Mam Diarra Bousso *daira*, not an association in honour of a nearby sheikh, who could give them *baraka* and protection, the president said in a warm and tender voice: 'Because we love Mam Diarra'.

Next time I came back to Mbacké (Autumn 1993) I saw the woman president again, I made new interviews with her, with the cashier and some of the secretaries and I attended two *daira* meetings. The picture became a little clearer. Finally, during my last stay in Mbacké December 1994 to March 1995 many questions were answered, although there still remain some obscure points concerning this religious association and its *raison d'être*. In my new interview with the president she said to my great surprise that the *daira* was mixed, there were both male and female members. But how could it be that men would like to attend a *daira* for Mam Diarra Bousso, the mystical mother figure who is venerated primarily by women? The president insisted, however, that there were in fact male participants. In all they were eighty women members, she said, and around thirty male members. All the women were from the same town quarter, she continued, and most of them were petty traders, mainly trading in cloth, fruit and toasted peanuts. The president herself had a son who was a tailor and the mother sold the dresses in Mbacké and in some neighbouring villages, which she visited occasionally. Before they traded with smuggled goods from the Gambia, but after the devaluation of the Franc CFA in January 1994, they would buy cloth in Touba, which is a freetown with duty-free goods, or in Dakar, and sell it in Mbacké. The young male participants had different professions, mostly tailors and artisans. They were all bachelors and earned some extra money from singing the *qasaids* for other people, 'volunteering' also in other *dairas* and at religious events occasionally. Their fame as good *qasaid* singers was well established in Mbacké.

Earlier the association used to meet each Friday, but because it was difficult for the men to come after the Friday prayer in the mosque to the *daira*, they had now changed the meetings to Monday afternoons. That is, the women gathered each Monday.

Once a month the fee was collected, the funds being absolutely central to the *daira's* activities and called 'the Calebass of Mam Diarra Bousso'. Half of the money was, as mentioned, set aside for the *magal* in Porokhane and there given to a Mam Diarra Bousso family representative (*Sokhna* Astou Boury Mbacké in Porokhane) while the other half of the money was used for transportation to the place of the pilgrimage and the food for the trip. The men did not attend every Monday meeting, but when they came they sang the religious songs of Sheikh Amadou Bamba (the *qasaids*) for the women. Nor did they make any contributions in money. The fee was low: the women paid CFA 300 each month (100 Franc CFA are equivalent to 1 Franc Francais). In January 1995 the fee was increased to CFA 500 due to higher prices for food and transport.

But why the men in the *daira*? 'We need the men', the president explained, 'for three reasons: for singing the *qasaids*, for heavy work we cannot do and for protection'. I would imagine they especially need the men for their yearly pilgrimage to Porokhane. They then go with the money and the bowls with prepared food. The money can easily be robbed and the bowls are heavy. It is also more respectable to go with men than with only women. 'To be only women, far from home, could be provoking', said the president; 'it is not said but it is like that'.

The Mam Diarra Bousso *daira* used to be both a religious association and a *mbotaye*, the form of association mentioned above, which gives contributions to the women for financing the feasts that accompany primarily marriages and name-givings. The same women were members in both associations. The women met each Saturday, but they did not collect money or cloth more than on the occasions needed. The sum on each occasion was CFA 1000. 'And what about the young men?', I wondered. The women said that they were also part of the *mbotaye*. 'But how could that be possible?' I was really astonished. Well, they were young men all of them and lacked the financial means for their marriages. As they helped the women to keep the *daira* going through their physical presence and singing the religious songs, the women tried to help them in cash and cloth as well when they had their rites-de-passage feasts. That was the reason for classifying them as 'participants' in the genuinely female association, traditionally for married women only.

The main purpose of the *daira* was and is participation in the Mam Diarra Bousso *magal* in Porokhane. Much time is spent in the meetings to plan and discuss the annual trip. Once the great event is over and the participants are back home, one meets to go through all the details of the pilgrimage and to inform the members, who did not join, about the *magal*. A special kind of beverage, tasting like bitter coffee, is served, called café Touba, which is considered typically Murid. The older ladies dominate the conversation at these meetings. The younger women sit together on mats in one part of the courtyard; the older ones occupy the central part of the yard and the young men, when they are present, gather around the amplifier in the back of the houseyard.

What are the attractions of the Mam Diarra Bousso *magal*? Besides having all the characteristics of a real big religious feast with a voluminous market attached to it, the handing over of the *addiyya*, the money collected during the past year, to *Sokhna* Astou Boury of the Bousso-Mbacké family and the *ziyara*, the visit to the holy places in Porokhane constitute the two most thrilling events of the *magal*. The absolutely most important part of the *ziyara* is the visit to the tomb (Wolof: *khabru*), where the pilgrim formulates wishes to Mam Diarra about what one really needs and wants. Other elements of the *ziyara* are the collection of 'holy' water from the well, and a visit to the places where Mam Diarra used to pound her millet and her son Sheikh Amadou Bamba used to crawl around in the sand before he learnt to walk. The mosque is visited both at night on the day of arrival and again for the afternoon prayer, as the second day of the *magal* usually is a Friday.[4]

The marketplace is another essential part of the *magal*. Friday morning is usually dedicated to visiting the market. The purchases are of two kinds; the women buy gifts which bring blessing to close family members, who have not been able to accompany the others on the pilgrimage, and they buy items, mostly cloth, for trading. In Porokhane the imported goods from the Gambia are sold duty-free and prices are generally lower than in Dakar. The only constraint is the customs, who tend to wait along the roads from Porokhane in order to stop the returning vehicles and look for the traders' duty-free goods, which then have to be paid for or left on the spot with the custom officials.

Thousands of people attend the *magal*, the atmosphere being pleasant, people looking happy to be there. Instead of just sitting in the marabout's house for hours as is the case during other *magals*, in Porokhane people move around. Most pilgrims appear relaxed and good-humoured during their tour around to the different activities and places of the *ziyara*. The pilgrims — men and women alike — imitate Mam Diarra pounding her millet by borrowing a mortar from the hands of the Bai Fall disciples,[5] who assist the visitors and ask for alms. The symbolic act of pounding, carried out also by male pilgrims, transgresses ordinary male norms. So does the imitation of Sheikh Amadou Bamba's crawling around in the sand as a child, which all the visitors smilingly do in the hope of getting some of the *baraka* of the place into their bodies and souls. This physical activity in combination with the longing for Mam Diarra Bousso's miraculous and mystical power of giving to oneself what one most of all needs and wants provides the *magal* in Porokhane with a special dimension of grace, pleasure and excitement.

In late 1994 only thirty women were actual members of the Mam Diarra Bousso *daira*. Out of this number, only seventeen had paid their fee, *addiyya*, and were therefore allowed to go on the pilgrimage, organized by the *daira* board. The *mbotaye* association had been dissolved because the president said the women did not pay to the *daira*, only to the *mbotaye*. This had caused trouble and conflicts among the members. The pilgrimage to Porokhane remained the main activity for the *daira*, but it seemed that interest in this was not so great among the younger women. The majority of women in the actual *daira* and among the pilgrims to Porokhane were older women — petty traders and grandmothers. All members except the cashier (who was enrolled in another *daira* for another marabout through her husband) were simultaneously members of another *daira*, called *Willaya* (Wolof: house) which venerated Sérigne Mbacké *Sokhna* Lô, a famous and popular sheikh in his fifties, living not far from Mbacké. On the Mam Diarra Bousso Monday meetings a special fee for him was charged from the members for his *addiyya*, the sum being CFA

50 weekly. Each year the members made the *magal* to his house in Darou Khoudoss. This was, thus, the answer to my wondering about how the women could live without the support and spiritual protection of a living marabout. He could provide his members with the longed for *baraka*. The women as well as the men could work for him when demanded by him or the *khalifa general*, and these favours would give people both religious blessing and merit (Wolof: *tiyaba*).

Sokhna[6] Salimatu Diallo, a Member of the Mam Diarra Bousso *Daira*[7]

Here follows a presentation of one pious member of the Mam Diarra Bousso *daira*. I have chosen her because she expressed herself so well, and seemed to enjoy talking about her religious life and practice. She is a 'typical' member in the sense that she is comparatively old in the eyes of the surrounding society, her children are grown up and she has passed that stage of her female life which is characterized mainly by hard work. She has both time and some money to dedicate to the *daira* activities. She now has no reason to be a *mbotaye* member, at least not in the town of Mbacké, where she lives just temporarily, as she is beyond reproductive age and no longer has any costs for namegiving rituals and parties nor marriages.

Sokhna Salimatu Diallo is almost fifty years old, she tells when being interviewed,[8] and of the ethnic group Fulani (Wolof: *Peul*). She is *geer* (non-caste, which is considered of superior status compared to the caste people) and Murid. She lives in a polygynous marriage in a village outside Mbacké, but has recently moved into her brother's house in town to take care of her old mother, who is blind and needs help.

Sokhna Salimatu is herself a mother of four children, she has never been to school but studied the Koran as a young girl. Her daily occupation is to sell oranges, which she buys in the Mbacké marketplace. This is a very small-scale business, which also runs more or less for something to do and as an excuse for sitting outside the house and chatting with the neighbours without being considered idle. Sometimes she even gives oranges away to the children without charging them. Her husband and sons do not like her petty trade activities. They say this is not something that a

Peul woman like her should do; this kind of trade is beneath her dignity and she does not need that marginal income. The only thing they could think of selling for a *Peul* woman was milk.

> When asked what she did the day before, she answered: Yesterday was monotonous as usual, because I did not do anything, really. It is the wife of my older brother who goes shopping in the marketplace and it is the domestic help who cleans up the house. I sat down outside in front of my table as soon as I got up and then I extended myself on my mat and I took my rosary to say my prayers. You know, now I am old and I take my rest and I follow nothing but the prescriptions of God.

Like the other members, *Sokhna* Salimatu is a member of both the Mam Diarra Bousso *daira* and the one of Sérigne Mbacké *Sokhna* Lô (in order to distinguish him from all other Sérignes Mbackés that are found in Senegal, the name of his mother is added to his). She has joined the Mam Diarra Bousso *daira* because she wants to 'approach God, do the *ziyaras* and also to come closer to my marabout'. She thinks that one gets much more blessing if one joins a religious association and together with the other members dedicates oneself to religious activities such as singing and listening to the religious songs and collecting money each month to prepare for the *magal*. Moreover, she said that she tried to lead a modest and pious life. As an example, she mentioned that she never went anywhere; 'you know, I have never attended a *tam-tam*[9] nor gone to a cinema, for I know that these activities will lead you on to bad roads; they distance you from God.' 'And what about blessing? How do you get it?' *Sokhna* Salimatu answered that the *barke* (blessing) begins with the parents, that is to say that the individual starts to have *barke* with her parents, by showing submission and most of all by helping them in all ways if one can, if one works and earns money, 'because it is thanks to them that one lives.' She continued:

> And when the marabout came and ordered his disciples to follow the *khalif's ndigeul* (order) to go to Khelkoum[10] then the whole *daira* went, because we have chosen Sérigne Mbacké *Sokhna* Lô as our sheikh. He is also a disciple of the *khalif*, so we had to obey the order of the marabout and that is why we all went and we stayed there for a week in order to do the agricultural work there. Certainly we will have blessing because

we worked for the marabout and in exchange we will have *barke,* which is the reward of the work.

Concerning the pilgrimage to Porokhane, *Sokhna* Salimatu had this to say:

I insist in going there each year because it is a holy place and because that is where the corpse of Mam Diarra Boussso rests. This was the fourth time I went to Porokhane (in 1995) thanks to God, for if it had not been for him I would never have put my feet there. You know, between Mbacké and Porokhane there are kilometres and kilometres, it is a long and tough trip, but if you really decide to go there, and when you believe in God the Merciful, one will arrive there whatever hardships one will encounter/face on the trip. The first time I went together with my husband with a horse and carriage. In spite of all the risks I decided to go like that. The other three times I have been going with the Mam Diarra Bousso *daira.*

In Porokhane I went to the Mam Diarra tomb first on Thursday and then on Friday again to make the *ziyara* and ask her for many things that I need in my life. The others went to the marketplace on Friday morning, for no matter whether the *magal* is in Porokhane, in Touba or in any other place, lots of traders come with their goods in order to earn some money. For example, in Porokhane lots of vendors came from the Gambia and sold towels, cloth, matches, jewellery, shoes - indeed, many things. But what interested me the most was the cloth. So I went to the market to buy myself a *khartoum* (a special kind of cotton cloth) to wear on the next magal and a loincloth for my mother-in-law as a gift, for I had no intention to go there for commercial purposes. When all of us had made our purchases we went together to *Sokhna* Astou Boury's room once again and together we sang the *qasaids* (she refers to the Mam Diarra Bousso songs) and talked about things concerning Porokhane. Around two o'clock in the afternoon we went to the mosque, still in the company of *Sokhna* Astou Boury to make the Friday prayer. As the *magal* was on the night between Thursday and Friday, this gave us a great occasion to pray together on Friday also, so this was really good luck for us. After the prayer we returned immediately to *Sokhna* Astou's house to prepare the departure for Mbacké. And even if the *magal* is exhausting I will always ask God to take me to Porokhane each year with the Mam Diarra Bousso *daira* and also to see to it that all Muslims who would like to go can do it.

Summing Up: Female Religious Participation — The Case of the Mam Diarra Bousso *Daira*

It is obvious that the Murid women need to organize themselves to be able to go to a *magal* like the one in Porokhane, particularly when they have no husband or family to join them. It is also obvious that these same women, who for ideological reasons are considered second-rate as Muslims in the most important rituals, need the presence and support of the young men to be able to keep a female *daira* like Mam Diarra Bousso going in a prestigious and attractive way. In this case young men are brought in to mediate between the female *daira* participants and the surrounding society. That the men are young and mostly not married makes them more accessible for the women; they would hardly get older, married men to come as 'helpers' in a female *daira*. That would certainly have been considered odd. The young men thus in a sense 'help women to holiness'. The *qasaids* can only be sung by the young men and they are heard widely from the President's house yard. These songs are in Arabic, and as mentioned written by the founder of the Muridiyya, Sheikh Amadou Bamba. The fact that the songs are based on citations from the Koran explains why women as impure beings cannot sing them. For the *daira* members it is good that not only the less holy and less prestigious songs about Mam Diarra Bousso, which the women sing themselves in Wolof, are presented. Without the men, the young girls' task would have been to sing for the women, as they did on those occasions when the men did not attend the meetings. Another important fact is related to the men's voices: they are expected to sing aloud and they certainly do, fortifying their voices by electronic equipment. The women, on the contrary, are expected to be silent, or in the case of the Mam Diarra Bousso songs, to sing them in a low voice, 'not to distract the men', as the saying goes.

In line with this, it can be said that women need men for their ritual purity; they need men as performers of Murid rituals for them. The singing of the *qasaids* is the main religious activity of a *daira*. Normally, women are not allowed to sing them, nor to dance to them.[11] Women should be the listeners. Women's lack of religious knowledge and of literacy makes them dependent on men who read prayers for them and interpret the legends about

Sheikh Amadou Bamba and his mother. Women also need men for the *baraka* that these songs give besides the prestige in the town's quarter where the women live (remember that most members are neighbours). The membership in the Sérigne Mbacké *Sokhna Lô daira* provides the women with male maraboutic blessing and the social security that a close-by living religious leader can offer. This is something they cannot get through their own *daira's* mystical figure, as Mam Diarra died about 130 years ago. Male mediation between a marabout and the women in the Murid brotherhood is not only the task of the husbands, who are not interested in letting the women penetrate too deeply into their domain. Young men could provide some of these services, traded against material help in the form of money and collective ritual services.

In the Murid case, the religious authority rests with the marabout. The leadership of the Mam Diarra Bousso *daira* is held by the President who has an important and influential position. Her greatest asset is her social network and her reputed piety. Also, she and the cashier have control over the money, which is collected in the Mam Diarra Bousso calebass. The President belongs to the group of non-caste (Wolof: *geer*) which is considered a superior group. The President is the patron for her *daira* members, mostly caste women of lower status (Wolof: *ñeeño*), who are her clients. They see her as a kind of social mother, whose many contacts with prestigious groups of the society and her connections with one or several marabouts can be of help. The President herself maintains links of mutual interest and dependence with the marabout of the *daira,* or in this case, with the *sokhnas* (women of maraboutic descent or married to a marabout) of the Bousso family.

The Bousso family needs an active President, as she provides them with members and *magal* visitors, who contribute to the image and the material resources of the Bousso family. And the President needs the members to maintain her position as a President - acting as a mother, who can 'protect' her clients/daughters. The participation of the women in the *daira* has to be seen from the Murid women's perspective. The women consider all the things that they do in connection with the *daira* as religious acts, which will render them *baraka* as well as *tiyaba*, religious merit. They do participate by their presence, by their work, by their organizational skills and by their financial contributions. Many of them, if not everybody, are devote; they like to hear the legends about the religious leaders and their mothers; they like the songs and the feasts; they attend the *magal* both because of its holiness and because of the possibilities to go away on an exciting excursion and prepare and eat good food and buy things in the marketplace. They like the *magal* as a social event; to dress up in new clothes and jewellery. The *daira* meetings are, besides the religious aspect, an occasion for social activities and a forum for the making of marriage strategies (M'Bow 1994).

Female Murid identity is, as already mentioned, linked to the participation in *dairas*, in *magals*, in the performance of the *ziaras,* in the preparation of food for the religious feasts, the organization of *gammous* and to the work and money they offer their marabouts. What I see as conserving women's position in Muridism is the current stress on female lack of purity, knowledge and blessing by the Islamic male activists - even if they give no importance to *baraka* - as well as by the Sufi marabouts and male disciples, who do pay attention to the blessing factor. Religious and gender ideas seem to constitute strong ideational structures, comparatively resistant to change and mutually fortifying each other. Still, of course, these 'tough' structures continuously adapt to all kinds of change in their surroundings and in so doing undergo many transformations. The whole phenomenon of a female *daira* like the one called Mam Diarra Bousso is a proof of such an adaptation to a new era, in which women are able to partly overcome their ideological, culturally constructed 'handicap' in religious life and in the society at large. They can do this, as we have seen, through involving young men in women's pious activities, trading men's protection, prestige and *baraka* against women's financial resources and ceremonial services. To reach that far, money, age and civil status must work together to make it possible for women to lead such activities. A good reputation for being pious, honest and comparatively well off opens up wide fields of religious and economic action for the women. Added to this, as the mother image has positive religious/ Sufi as well as secular connotations in Senegal, the Murid women

are especially motivated to become members in a *daira* which
venerates the memory of an ideal and almost sacred mother figure
like Mam Diarra Bousso.

Notes

1. An abbreviated version in French of this article was
    published in *Transforming Female Identities: Women's
    Organizational Forms in West Africa*, Uppsala: The Nordic
    Africa Institute, 1997.
2. Hierarchically ranked ascribed status groups, based on
    professions.
3. Villalón describes in his book on Islamic society and state
    power what he calls 'a unique case in Fatick of an
    all-women's daira which claims no affiliation with any other
    order' (1995: 162). In New York among the female Murid
    immigrants there exist Mam Diarra Bousso dairas for women
    only. So it seems realistic to think that one could find several
    'unique cases' of female religious associations of different
    kinds but built on the maraboutic system as a whole.
4. The date for the *magal* differs a little from one year to
    another, which makes it possible to choose a Thursday.
5. The Bai Fall disciples belong to a ´subgroup´ of the
    Muridiyya. They are followers of Sheikh Ibrahima Fall,
    Sheikh Amadou Bamba's most well-known and charismatic
    disciple.
6. This woman is called *sokhna* even if she is neither a daughter
    or a wife of a marabout. The title indicates that she is a
    married woman, a mother, and a grandmother, of a certain
    age and status in the society. This is publicly confirmed by
    calling her *sokhna*, just as the president of the *daira* is called
    Sokhna Maimouna.
7. The real name and some biographical details of the informant
    have been changed to protect her anonymity.
8. The interview was made in Wolof by my assistant Muskeba
    Fofona, Department de Sociologie, Université de Saint Louis,
    and translated by her into French.
9. *Tam-tams* are afternoon gatherings, held outside the house,
    where people dance and amuse themselves, accompanied by

drums and music, the latter mostly played on a cassette-player with big amplifiers.

10. Khelkoum refers to a huge 'forêt classifié' (protected forest) which was situated in central Senegal. The *khalif general* ordered all the Murid disciples in 1992 to cut down the forest, which had been preserved and protected since the time of the French colonialists. Since then, he annually gives an order to the disciples to go to Khelkoum for a period of about five days to harvest the millet that is cultivated where the forest used to grow.

11. To say, as I do, that women cannot sing the *qasaids*, may be too categorical a statement, which I had better mitigate. There are many exceptions to this rule or norm. As a matter of fact many marabouts do not mind the women's singing; others do not allow it, while they admit that women sing the *qasaids* separately, with no men present. There is also a generational difference among the Murid marabouts concerning their attitude to this question. The older ones maintain that women should be silent, while some younger marabouts and men trained in reading the Koran and its interpretations say it is clearly stated by the Prophet that women should pray and sing, just like the men do. According to my own experience in Mbacké, Murid women do not sing the Sheikh Amadou Bamba *qasaids* together with the men or alone.

References

Buitelaar, M. (1993), *Fasting and Feasting in Morocco. Women's Participation in Ramadan,* Oxford/Providence: Berg.

Copans, J. (1980), *Les marabouts de l'arachide. La confrérie mouride et les paysans du Senegal,* Paris: L'Harmattan.

Coulon, C. (1988), 'Women, Islam and Baraka' in C. Coulon and D. Cruise O'Brien (eds), *Charisma and Brotherhood in African Islam,* Oxford: Clarendon Press.

Coulon,C. and O. Reveyrand (1990), 'Islam au feminin: Sokhna Magot Diop: cheikh de la confrérie mouride (Senegal)', *Travaux et documents no 25,* Bordeaux: Centre d'Étude d'Afrique Noire.

Creevey, L. (1992), 'The Sword and the Veil: Islam and Women in Senegal', unpublished manuscript.

Diop, M.C. (1981), 'Fonctions et activités des dahira mourides urbains (Senegal)', *Cahiers d'Etudes Africaines*, Villes au microscope.

Ly, Boubacar, (no year indicated): 'L'honneur et les valeurs morals dans les sociétés ouolof et toucouleur du Senegal', Etude de sociologie, thèse pour le doctorat de troisième cycle de sociologie, L'université de Paris.

Magassouba, M. (1985), *L'islam au Senegal — Demain les mollahs?* Paris: Karthala.

March, K.S. and R. Taqqu (1982), 'Women's Informal Associations and the Organizational Capacity for Development', paper, Cornell University: Rural Development Committee, Center for International Studies.

M'Bow, P. (1994), Les femmes dans les associations réligieuses en milieu urbain', MS thesis.

O'Brien, D.C. (1971), *The Mourides of Senegal: The Political and Economic Organization of an Islamic Brotherhood*, Oxford: Clarendon Press.

O'Brien, D.C. (1988), 'Charisma Comes to Town', in D.C. O'Brien and C. Coulon (eds), *Charisma and Brotherhood in African Islam*, Oxford: Clarendon Press.

Rosander, E.E. (ed.) (1997), *Transforming Female Identities: Women's Organizational Forms in West Africa*, Uppsala: Nordic Africa Institute.

Villalón, L.A. (1995), *Islamic Society and State Power in Senegal: Disciples and Citizens in Fatick*, Cambridge: Cambridge University Press.

Chapter 7

Reconstruction of Islamic Knowledge and Knowing: A Case of Islamic Practices among Women in Iran

Zahra Kamalkhani

This chapter attempts to give some understanding of women's religious activities in the context of Islamic tradition and modernity in Iran. By modernity of Islamic practices, I mean a search for new knowledge, a positive stance toward innovation and a quest for social and political development which reshape tradition. My view supports those who argue that contemporary Islamization represents a particular brand of modernity rather than a reaction against it (Caplan 1987, Eickelman 1992, Horvatich 1994). This article shows some of the consequences of this process for women's social and political mobility in today's Iran.

A common explanation for the rise of Islamization in general and the Islamic segregation of the sexes in public spheres in particular is that it expresses a desire to return to a traditional essentialist Islam of the past as well as being against social and economic modernity. Furthermore, among conventional scholar- ship the Islamic traditions of the past are often understood as religious marginalization of women, patriarchal domination, with the female segregated and veiled. These classical Middle East cultural elements are often viewed as social symbols of political and economic subordination and segregation by Western observers. But these observers commonly ignored the existence of women's active religious role. It would be too facile to describe the return of the women to religious orthodoxy as simply reactionary or imitating male culture. In my view such a line of approach neither gives us a comprehensive understanding of contemporary Muslim women's Islamic awareness, nor provides an understanding of practices and the innovative nature of Islamic knowledge. Looking at the development of women's life situations under the new economic and political turbulence in many Muslim societies, a fresh perspective is required to give us knowledge about the increasing number of women entering into Islamic orthodoxy and intellectualism.

One often notices that the discussion of what is 'Islamic' is restricted to the culture of the male elite and their participation in the movement. Women's relationship to the mainstream of Islamic practices remains largely unrecorded and has not received adequate attention in terms of their contribution to Islamic awareness and Islamic nationalism in Iran. However, there is a new Islamic zeal developing in relation to women, which is evident in a female Islamic movement and involvement. Many aspects of women's life situations have become the province of the Islamists by means of educational control and religious involvement. In particular, this has affected the arena of traditional religious rituals, the religious socialization of the new generation and educational opportunities for the young (Eickelman 1992; Yaganeh 1993; Higgens & Ghaffari 1994).[1]

Below I first give some examples of Iranian women's religious activity and secondly, discuss the way in which local religious life becomes a locus for the reproduction of new Islamic meanings and acquires a political dimension.

Women's Religious Activity in 1989

As part of my Ph.D programme and for the purpose of anthropological observation, I planned to follow women's social life in post-revolutionary Iran in 1989. Although my original research proposal was not concerned with the study of women's religious life, by the second day of my arrival I had learned that women were engaged in something of importance that had escaped my attention till then.

On that occasion I participated in a religious meeting in which the entire Koranic verse *anam*, the so called *khatm-e anam* (K: 6) was recited. That was a ritual of annual memory (*sar-sal*) of one of my relatives, where two female preachers were in charge and my relatives were host. There I met another relative who invited me to her Koran meetings (*jales-e Koran*) in which she was in charge of the Koranic lessons. This kind of meeting is open to the public and a place to meet other relatives, friends and neighbours. A few days later I went to her Koran lessons which were attended by twenty women, some with their school-age daughters or young sons, in the sitting room of a private home. I learned about other religious meetings (*rowzeh-e zananeh*) where a different host and a female preacher were in charge and which were carried on in different parts of the town.

I participated in several of these Koran meetings on a regular basis over the period March-August 1989 (covering the Muslim lunar months of *Ramazan, Shawwal, Dhul-Qa'adah, Dhul-Hijjah, Muharram* and *Safar*). After attending one meeting I was soon accepted as a participant in a series of meetings where religious rituals were carried out by one or more female preachers on public holy days or family religious rituals that were arranged every day during the month of fasting (Ramazan) and the mourning months of Muharram and Safar. Some religious meetings followed the Islamic calendar, others were performed on auspicious days such as Thursday evening for reciting of *nodbeh*,[2] or Friday morning for reading the blessed text of *komyl*,[3] or *joshan-kabir* from the Shi'i book of Mafatieh.

These religious meetings were performed at specific times of the day, such as the early morning or evening, and in specific months of the year such as Muharram and Ramazan. The annual meetings were on specific days such, as the commemoration of the second Shi'i Imam Hasan, and of his brother, the third Imam Husain. The most blessed days were considered to be the commemoration days for Imam Ali, the Prophet's son-in-law and cousin, and the day on which it is believed that Muhammad nominated Imam Ali as his successor (*aid-e ghadir*), a legitimate successor in the Shi'i view. Other religious meetings were those celebrating the last day of the month of fast (*Eid-e fitr*), and the day of sacrifice (*Eid-e ghorban*). On each of these occasions Koran meetings are arranged in private houses. Motivated meetings were generally carried out throughout the whole year, but it was thought that the flow of grace (*barakat*) would be greatest for one´s religious activity during holy months and days/nights.[4]

Women's Religious Activity in 1994

During my second period of fieldwork, during the three Islamic lunar months of *Muharram, Safar* and *Rabi-ul-Awwal* (June-August 1994) I participated in the same local female religious meetings. There I came to know about a new religious meeting, recommended by one of my female informants, who said it was a place where discussions attained a higher Islamic standard than at the regular meetings I used to attend. These meetings were arranged in a newly opened public religious house named after the prominent third Shi'i Imam Husain (Hosyneh) and donated as *waghf* to the community by its owner a religiously oriented elderly childless woman from a well-off religious family. Hosyneh is a mosque-like public religious hall where religious meetings, communal prayers and sermons are performed. There were three preachers of different rank who gave daily speeches and were in charge of ritual on different religious themes. One started at seven in the morning with preaching and instruction on problems of ritual and was followed by the higher ranked preacher who often arrived with several books in her hands to recommend to the audience and the Koran commentary (*tafsir*). Finally it was the turn of the ritual expert who performed the religious tragic and narrative song (*noheh*) about one of the prominent Shi'i imams. This meeting was arranged at the expense of the host throughout the months of Muharram and Safar.

On the second day of the month of Safar I was on my way to the *rowzeh* and before I entered the house I could hear the voice of the preacher very clearly outside, reciting and singing a sorrowful song (*noheh*) in honour of the twelfth Sh'ii imam; Imam Mahdi; the awaited messianic figure.[5] Loud-speakers have been commonly used since the revolution and indeed there is often a large crowd at female religious meetings; nevertheless, it surprised me in light of my experience from other Koran meetings where traditional preachers were in charge, but they usually made sure that their voices were not heard outside the hall. Generally, it is forbidden to let men hear the voices of women reciting the Koran and there was a conservative view in this regard among the ritual experts. Later on I found that the song was a popular greeting text (*ziyarat*) called Al-Yasin, performed by a guest preacher. There the narrative of the story about the Imam Mahdi in a mourning song created a strong emotional performance.

When the meeting finished I was able to approach the preacher who had performed the sorrowful song. She was a young student in the final phase at a high-level girls' religious school in Shiraz. I expressed my surprise that her loud and effective performance could be heard outside by the pedestrians (meaning, by men). She insisted that it was necessary to give merit to all her listeners on such a holy day. To her the religious message was given priority over gender segregation and the taboo on women's religious voices being heard in public. This is viewed more conservatively by traditional preachers who explicitly ensure that men do not hear their voices. A few days later at the meeting I approached a stall which used to sell Islamic cassettes of male clergy and Islamic books, and was able to buy the worship *do'a* of Al-Yasin, which had been performed the other day by the Islamic student. This was the first time I heard the recorded voice of a female preacher. Later I learned that there were other cassettes that I could borrow after becoming a member of the preacher's private library which was located in her home.

All these performances have meant an accumulation of articulated Islamic knowledge and a sense of cultural innovation. First, to a new graduate preacher the importance of religious intention has become an alternative solution to some of the taboos on women's public religious acts. Second, the importance of the development of Islamic ritual practices lies in the fact that such religious meetings and this form of family financial endowment have become powerful and popular. However, these forms of female religious activities and family economic contributions are not entirely new, but to some extent they occurred in the pre-revolutionary period.

What is significantly new is the way religious knowledge is mediated to local audiences by popular means. My religious companion reminded me that the host couple of the new women's Islamic house (Hosyneh) was the same who during the former shah's regime presented a golden door to the shrine of the Shi'i third Imam (Imam Husain) in Najaf in Iraq. She said this was a proof that they were always earnest believers. That showed clearly the extension of communal religious performance and the integration of female Islamic experts into more public Islamic arenas. It was also noticeable that the large number of learned and young seminary leaders often attracted bigger audiences than their former teachers or traditional local preachers.

In order to explore further some of the modern social dimensions of traditional female religious activity, I will first provide some information on the customary practices and initiation forms of these Koran meetings.

Initiation of Religious Rituals

The women's religious meetings were often held to fulfil a vow (*nazr*) expressed through sponsorship of a saint or the needy. For example, a woman may vow that if a particular request is granted or a personal or family difficulty remedied, she will sponsor a specific kind of religious ceremony. These votive meetings were different according to personal desire and ritual form and were initiated by women of various social classes. They were open to women and were often arranged privately in homes or in one of the religious public buildings such as the Islamic school or colleges and the female religious house (Hosyneh). Female networks of kinsfolk, friendship or neighbours, mobilized participants from one meeting or a local neighbourhood (*mahaleh*) to another. Some of these religious meetings which were started during my first fieldwork period March to August 1989, still carried on the annual Muharram meetings in my second period of fieldwork between June and August 1994.

Meetings were also arranged in order to receive blessings to protect or enhance the host's health and wealth. This type of religious meeting is often organized on a regular basis, but is most frequent during the holy days and months. They are arranged to honour promises given in return for the happy completion of a wish. Often several female co-organizers shared the tasks of serving participants with drinks taking care not to miss any of them. They expect to receive a gift of merit in return for such a religious work. This type of task is considered to be an honourable religious work earning religious merit (*sawab*), not least for those young female religious students who stayed in the yards to sell the religious books of prominent clergy and Islamic speeches and lessons on cassettes to those attending. For the host and co-organizer it was mainly celebrating a fulfilled vow of family issues and merit-making which was expected to bring prosperity in this world, or after death to oneself and other close relatives in the next. The more expensive rituals included one comprising a communal meal in honour of the Shi'i martyr, brother of the third Imam Husain. The large votive communal meal was usually given by wives of affluent businessmen and was seldom initiated among lower middle-class families due to high food prices.

Religious meetings may be divided into three significant parts: 1) Reciting the holy verses either from the Koran or Mafatie;[6] 2) Exegesis of Koran (*tafsir*), 3) Narrative of women's lessons of worship (*masaleh-go'i*) from the book of solutions to everyday problems (*Resaleh halol-masaleh*).[7]

The women in charge of rituals were preachers, either graduates of a theological school (*hyozeh* or *maktab*), those brought into such a career as a result of religiously learned parents, or by having a clergy husband. For a woman to become a religious leader, knowledge of the Koran is needed of which a minimum is to be able to recite one of the popular holy verses for example *komyl*, *nodbeh* or *anam*, and to give lessons on obligatory prayers. However, it may not be necessary to have a deep knowledge of Arabic or a religious background through descent to become a leader of Koran meetings. For instance, the lowest rank of preacher is that of the so-called *Anami* — a title given to one who can recite the popular Koran verse of *anam*, as explained to me by informants. No matter how limited one's knowledge of the Koran, being a religious leader brings income and an independent job. The income earned by these female religious experts varied between several hundred and a thousand tomans, depending on the significance of the occasion and the generosity of the host. To compare this sum often amounted to more than the wage of an average teacher at a state school.

For those attending the meeting, participation entails both social and spiritual experiences, spending time with female friends or co-religious seminarians (*ham-jalesi*). While the preacher earns respect and income and furthers her spiritual career, those attending the meetings expect to earn religious merit for reciting the Koran and initiating vows. The atmosphere of the meetings was spiritual, relaxed, friendly and flexible — some following a routine of reciting and chanting and others relating more of the tradition of the Prophet, commentary on the Koran and reciting prayers.

Political Dimension of Koran Meetings

Those female preachers who were highly educated attracted larger crowds than the more traditional and less educated preachers in 1994. They were popular for giving a high standard of Islamic talk and realistic instruction in religious matters; they were identified as highly knowledgeable (*alem*), spiritual and skilful speakers. They could attract large attendances across social categories including students, schoolgirls and higher middleclass women. Female preachers are ranked by their followers as good speakers according to their knowledge of the Koran, Arabic language, their form of *tafsir* and how emotional they are in performing religious song (*noheh*). They accept pupils and university students as private students for lessons in the Koran. The popularity of the teacher has much to do with the Islamic state's compulsory demands for knowledge of the Koran, basic prayers and Islamic ideology on the part of those trying to get access to university or entering a civil service employment. Demands for higher Islamic knowledge promoted knowing and reciting the Koran from being a traditional interest among neighbourhood housewives and older local women in pre-revolutionary times to being the core of the national school curriculum and university studies today.

There are characteristic differences among female preachers. Some project a stronger association with the Islamic state, according to local categories of being *hezbullahi*, while others show no concern for daily politics. By following my *co-rowzeh* goers or going on my own from one religious meeting to another, it became clear to me that the politically oriented *hezbullahi* preacher made repeated references to women's religious modesty, their duty to cover themselves and adopt modest behaviour in conservative ways, whereas the politically neutral one (*bi-taraf*) took a more moderate view.

The preacher Mostafi was the one who raised the Islamic state's particular concern over veiling in most of her speeches in public places or at private homes in 1989. Through story-telling and reciting words from the Koran she sought to illustrate the Islamic ideals and framework of meaning. Let me give a few examples of the way in which she communicated her religious lessons at two different meetings.

The first one was the case of a widow who arranged an annual memorial Koran meeting of (*khatm-e anam*) for her husband in June 1989. Relatives both distant (including me) and close as well as friends and neighbours attended. In such a meeting the preacher is in charge and the Koran chapter of *Anam* is read thoroughly by several attendants. The preacher frequently interrupted her reading of the Koran to offer *tafsir* whenever there was mention of the terms for external and internal enemies (*monafeghin*) given in the Koran. She carefully used the opportunity to criticize the 'new Islamic veiling' of those women who were wearing thin stockings and the fashionable Islamic suit (*mantu*).[8] After the ceremony, the initiator of the *rowzeh* complained that she was very disappointed, and that the memorial ceremony for her husband had been used for political ends, which was an insult to his memory. The domain of family Islamic ritual activity has become an arena for internal social and political discourses of 'true' and 'false' identity of Muslim women.

Criticizing the inconsistent behaviour and distorted practice of 'Islamic' veiling among women, the preacher Mostafi repeatedly requested 'proper' veiling and gave lessons on its correct application. She often criticized women who adopted full cover for *rowzeh* and a loose cover outside in the streets, as being unconcerned about their prospects for the next world. Her remarks were directed at the contradictory behaviour of middle-class veiled women who changed veil from one occasion to another. Such changes and the adoption of contemporary fashionable styles of covering garment were considered worldly (*donyavi*), which was associated with the kind of behaviour classified as 'dolly'; — i.e. artificial, exhibitionist, provocative, and Westernized. This reflected irrationality and materialism which should be avoided even in the private sphere in interaction with bachelor male relatives. She often accused those women of undermining the

Islamic revolution ideology with improper covering and repeatedly saluted the Prophet Muhammad and his family, requesting participants to send blessing also to the leader of the revolution (*rahbar-e enghelab*) and his successor (*nayeb-imam*). Although a 'true' religious covering might seem unattractive in the present, it would bring rewards in the long after-life. According to preacher Mostafi, women wearing a proper *chador* (full length veil) despite the warmth and discomfort involved, displayed the quality of their social tolerance, the firmness of their faith and their superiority in worldly matters (March 1989). To her, 'true' female Islamic identity was defined by restrictive covering of body and hair and reserved social behaviour.

The political objective became apparent in the course of such religious speeches. Requesting participants to send loud blessings (*salvat*) at the end of a religious meeting was another example of political differences between preachers. During my first field work after the Iran-Iraq war in March 1989, the dominant themes at the end of each *rowzeh* were the blessing of martyrs, Islamic state fighters (*razmandegan-e Islam*) and demanding ill fortune for those acting as internal and external enemies of Islam (*monafeghin*).

A preacher could be identified by some of her students as being affiliated to the state's Islamic policy, *hezbullahi*, if after each sermon she called for a special merit to the leader of the revolution Imam Khomeini (*imam-e umat*), to his successor Khameini (*nayeb-e imam*) and to prime minister Rafsanjani. A preacher was known as neutral (*bi-taraf*) who extended the *salvat* to not more than the leader of the revolution (*imam-khomeini*). To participants this meant that the preacher avoided political issues but gave her recognition of the central figure of the revolution to avoid any problem for her work.

The *hezbullahi*'s leader used veiling and showed support to the Islamic state by using both personal and community idioms to signal being a 'true' Muslim.

Disseminating Islamic Learning through Mass Education

Since the Iranian revolution in 1979, it appears that political and socio-religious reforms have been transforming some aspects of the cultural 'tradition,' by reshaping former secular structures of the society with Islamic norms and values into the post-revolutionary religious, political and social reform system. At the time of my first fieldwork in Iran in 1989, it was evident that girls' religious education had become a central mechanism for the transmission of Islamic learning and political resistance among young women. The former religious schools and local Islamic activity had increased in size and numbers five years later in 1994. For example, a girls' religious school which was established in 1973 was converted to a theological college for training female preachers and ritual leaders in 1994. Muslims traditionally prize the search for knowledge and learning idealized in the Persian saying 'from cradle to grave seek knowledge'. Today, religious knowledge of a high standard including Arabic, prayers and jurisprudence (*fegheh*), have become a mark of the standard of one's faith *and* a social requisite for obtaining a job or passing academic exams.

After more than a decade, the Islamic state in Iran has been able to launch educational reforms which have resulted in building up a system of Islamic universities, colleges and religious schools[9] whose graduates acquire a broader religious knowledge, which subsequently speeds up access to job opportunities. This development is part of the process that has resulted in the production of new religious meaning and identity within the recognized frame of the society in which women are mobilized rather than marginalized.

The Islamic state aims to disseminate Islamic knowledge that may break down the classical dividing boundary between popular Islam and textual Islam. The Islamic state adopts the unity of education and Islamic knowledge as an important strategy for developing the Islamic national identity of both men and women. The Islamic Republic has formulated a series of direct and indirect policies on women's social participation in national politics, education and employment, through which women are to be incorporated into the nationalist movement as, for example, Islamic teachers and educated preachers. In addition, the relatives of those who gave their lives for their religious community (martyrs), associated male or female members of religious state organs such as the Islamic construction forces (*basiji*) and the

Islamic guards (*sepahi*), are also rewarded by the state in economic policy and educational recruitment (Habibi 1989). The martyr's relatives are promoted as first class citizens and get access to higher social welfare and better jobs. Twenty to thirty per cent of university places and higher standard schools are reserved for male and female relatives of such groups.

The development of the educational system by means of moral and political forces has been one of the prime concerns of the regime in Teheran since the revolution in 1979. The growth of Islamic literacy through various means of education and the transmission of knowledge in nurseries, school, university curricula, customary Koran courses, religious seminaries and the mass media have intermingled with distinctive forms of knowledge consisting of traditional, ideological, intellectual and textual knowledge under a subject called Islamic science (*ma'ref-e islami*).

Concluding Remarks

My approach to Islamic ways of knowing among women has described a form of knowledge by considering two issues: 1) customary religious learning and 2) postrevolutionary reformulation of Islamic mass education. Firstly, it is clear that women's exclusive Koran meetings in local areas and as part of family rituals, represent an Islamic core arena where women mobilize and display distinctive religious authoritative roles. Secondly, the Islamic elite and Islamists have influenced deliberately the content of these customary female rituals.

The development of local religious activity shows that the ways of learning Islam have changed from being a textual knowledge only accessible to a few cleric families or Islamic scholars, to include broader social categories crossing class, age and gender boundaries. The Islamic learning and knowing include both the process of every day experiential practices and state-based institutionalized teaching. Such a dual learning approach has empowered both contemporary Islamic intellectualism and has created new loci for political mobilization.

Academic Islamic scholarship focuses mostly on the textual and normative tradition of Islam. That is considered as superior knowledge, a 'great tradition' to use a Redfield term. Since the superiority of the 'great tradition' classically has been embodied by public and scholarly tradition, most scientific reports about Islamic beliefs and practices concern male religious tradition, not female participants and religious experts.

The traditional nature of Islamic female knowledge has developed from being publicly invisible and personal to being a focal point of national Muslim identity building under the Islamic Republic in Iran. We need to achieve a better understanding of the role that Islamic text and literacy play in daily experience and not draw an artificial boundary between what people read and what they believe or practice in everyday life. The traditional Islamic knowledge promoted through familiar religious events and formal national education plays a crucial role in the modern political economy of Islamic Iran. The compulsory orthodox lessons such as the perfect recitation of the Koran, understanding its meaning and knowing the ritual of prayers, dealing with death, fast, ablution, Friday and communal prayer, Islamic philosophy and so on, are regarded as a discrete subject to be taught from a Muslim mature age (for girls nine for boys twelve) under the national educational reforms. Modern Islamic education in contemporary Iran gives a simultaneous flow of traditional Islamic knowledge and interpretation of its present-day practices. We can not ignore that in the modern Islamic world, female students are increasingly aware of global political forces through the information apparatus of the state. This may foster the forces of resistance and encourage a new Islamic consciousness among young and educated women. Entering into political debates and discussions on anti-imperialism opens doors to the public arena and religio-professional careers.

In contemporary Iran many aspects of women's life situations have become the province of the Islamist both by means of control and active involvement; in particular, this has affected the arena of women's traditional religious rituals, their socialization and education. The so-called 'popular' Islam often identified with the nature of beliefs among ordinary Muslims (in particular women), has become interwoven with organized higher education and re-articulated both in the local and national context. The establishment of new theological schools and religious curricula and the extension of customary religious arenas and events has brought women more than ever into the active religious field. For me it was a matter of considerable surprise to discover several new public religious arenas, new mosques, regular religious meetings in private homes and even two new shrines in my local city in 1994. Such changes seemed to have developed in the period between my first and second fieldwork in 1994, when the merit of giving religious lessons seemed to have increased even more. Women in general have become more religiously and politically visible in the private as well as in the public arenas, through the customary channels of religious gatherings and through teaching in state institutions including schools (semi-secular and religious), universities. mosques and Islamic cultural centres.

Anthropologists need to pay greater attention to the role of persistent traditional learning and its reformulation via the local religious spheres and events in the national and global setting. In present-day Iran, the Muslim intellectuals and moderate theologians responsible for the state ideological structure, encourage women to take an Islamic role as educated people and display their Islamic loyalty to the state, community and family more publicly. Women's presence in educational institutions was regarded as an urgent political need and a modern policy for Muslim nation-building (see also Paidar 1995: 312). This line of encouragement provided them religious reward and integration as active believers in the context of competition in a constrained market for economic and employment opportunities.

The Islamic Republic imposed a reconstructed national educational system for the Islamization of society, but its popularity and strength are not solely dependent upon that. The interconnection of both traditional Koran meetings, practical experiences of Islamic learning and recent female Islamic theology training has brought about a strong sense of cultural accretion and an intertwining of classical boundaries of textual and popular Islamic knowledge. Thus the women provide links between customary religious practices and the new educational institutions. To me, the nature of Islamism represents a reunion of various modern elements with a traditional female religious fluidity and a state of socio-economic modernity. In this process the forgotten Islamic culture of women is brought into focus and confronts new roles defined in terms of Islamic Republic precepts.

Notes

1. Although it is difficult to determine the exact number of women involved in higher education, according to Higgens there were five times as many female students at the college level in 1990-91 as in 1977 (Higgens in Higgens & Ghaffari 1994: 32).
2. A verse of Mafatieh that is an appeal to the Imam Mahdi or Imam-Zaman, the awaited messianic figure among the Shi'i community of Twelvers.
3. A verse said to be named after one of Imam Ali's followers called Komyl, and full of merit for it forgives sin.
4. *Arbein, tasoa and Ashora* are among the most popular religious Shi'i days when taking and receiving meals was certain and for that reason my host did not prepare lunch at her house.
5. It is believed that the twelvth Shi'i Imam who went into occultation in AD 874, will return back to his Muslim community at the end of the world when people's lives are imbued with injustice.
6. Mafatieh or Mafatieh-il jenan is a Shi'i book of prayers. It means a key to paradise, and it consists of a collection of sacred verse of the Prophet collected first by Imam Ali, then by his successors and finally by Abas-Qumi.
7. The edition used in 1989 was a collection of statements by Khomeini.
8. The latest fashions were tight at the time and considered to be provocative, for they clearly revealed the shape of the body to men in contrast to the true Islamic style, which should be simple, loose and non-provocative.
9. For a description of male religious schools in Quom see Thaiss 1979, Fischer 1980.

References

Antoun, R. (1989), *Muslim Preacher in the Modern World: A Jordanian Case Study in Comparative Perspective*, Princeton: Princeton University Press.

Berkey, J.P. (1991), 'Women and Islamic Education', in N. Keddie & B. Baron (eds), *Women in Middle Eastern History,* London: Yale University Press.

Bourdieu, P. & J.C. Passeron (1977), *Reproduction in Education, Society and Culture*, Beverly Hills and London Sage.

Caplan, L. (1987), 'Introduction', *Studies in Religious Fundamentalism,* London: Macmillan.

Eickelman, D. (1985), *Knowledge and Power in Morocco*, Princeton: Princeton University Press.

Eickelman, D. (1992), 'Mass Higher Education and the Religious Imagination in Contemporary Arab Societies', *American Ethnologist*, vol. 19, no. 4, 643-55.

Fernea, R. & E. Fernea (1972), 'Variation in Religious Observance among Islamic Women', in N. Keddie (ed.), *Scholars, Saints and Sufis*, Berkeley: California University Press.

Fischer, M. (1980), 'Madrasa: Style and Substance', *Iran, From Religious Dispute to Revolution*, Cambridge: Mass. Harvard University Press.

Habibi, N. (1989), 'Occupations and Opportunities in the Islamic Republic of Iran: A Case Study in the Political Screening of Human Capital in the Islamic Republic of Iran', in *The Journal of the Society for Iranian Studies*, vol. XXII, no. 4, 19-46.

Kamalkhani, Z. (1993), 'Women's Everyday Religious Discourse in Iran', in H. Afshar (ed.), *Women in the Middle East; Perception, Reality and Struggles for Liberation*, 85-95. London: Macmillan series.

Higgens, P. & P.Sh. Ghaffari (1994), 'Women's Education in the Islamic Republic of Iran', in M. Afkhami & E. Friedl (eds), *In the Eye of the Storm*, London: I.B. Tauris.

Horvatich P. (1995), 'Ways of knowing Islam', *American Ethnologist*, vol. 21, no. 4, 811-26.

Piscatori, J.P. (1989), *Islam in the Political Process,*

Paidar, P. (1995), *Women and the Political Process in Twentieth Century Iran*, Cambridge: Cambridge University Press.

Redfield, R. (1953), *Peasant Society and Culture*, Chicago: University of Chicago Press.

Tapper, N. (1983), 'Gender and Religion in a Turkish Town: A Comparison of Two Types of Formal Women's Gatherings', in P. Holden (ed.), *Women's Religious Experience*, London: Croom Helm.

Thaiss, G. (1979), 'The Conceptualization of Social Change through Metaphor', *Journal of Asian and African studies*, 8/1-2, 1-13.

Yaganeh, N. (1993), 'Women, Nationalism and Islam in Contemporary Political Discourses in Iran', *Feminist Review*, no.44.

Index